Beautiful

in God's eyes

He has made
everything beautiful
in its time.

Ecclesiastes 3:11, NKJV

REVIEW AND HERALD® PUBLISHING ASSOCIATION

Since 1861 | www.reviewandherald.com

Compiled by Penny Wheeler
Edited by Ardis Stenbakken
Cover design by Bryan Gray / Review and Herald® Design Center
Interior design by Emily Ford / Review and Herald® Design Center
Cover art by © Thinkstock.com
Typeset: Minion Pro 11/13
Interior photos: © Thinkstock.com

PRINTED IN U.S.A.

18 17 16 15 14   5 4 3 2 1

Library of Congress Control Number: 2014932028

ISBN 978-0-8280-2739-7

Introduction

Do you think that you're beautiful? Most of us don't. Well, maybe once or twice a year we do, when we've put a lot of effort into our clothes and makeup and then someone we care about says, "Wow! You look good." For a few minutes we actually believe it, but then the little voice in our heads says *Don't be ridiculous,* and suddenly we're painfully aware that we're too skinny or too tall or too heavy . . . or too *something*!

Open this book and become acquainted with some women who are pretty much like you and me—executive assistants, teachers, servers, homemakers, nurses, and more. But each has learned to recognize that now and again God steps into their ordinary days and gives them an unexpected blessing.

Karen often finds herself doing the one little thing that no one else has time for. She calls that "gap-filling," and she's good at it. Jill acted on the thought to give a favorite coffee mug to a woman she works with, not knowing that she was facing some serious medical tests and that the simple gesture meant everything to her.

Have you done everything you knew how to do and things still didn't work out? Jayne did. Let her share what happened *then.*

Are you dealing with a debilitating illness? Have circumstances forced you to leave everything you hold dear? Then you'll be encouraged by Lilya's experience. God touched her with exactly what she needed.

Lying on a table for a breast biopsy, Julie says she was praying up "a tornado" when she heard the words "Praise Me." So she did. She began singing, and her fear disappeared.

And then there's the tired mother who learned that sometimes what you need most of all is to laugh.

This book is packed with stories—some simple, some heart-wrenching, some as miraculous and ordinary as an answered prayer. Open these pages and become acquainted with women just like you. They love, they laugh, they fear, they cry. And in ways both profound and simple God touched each life.

Look over their shoulders. Hear their stories. And learn to recognize just how beautiful you, too, are in the eyes of God.

Penny Estes Wheeler

> He has made everything beautiful in its time.
>
> Ecclesiastes 3:11, NKJV.

You should clothe yourselves instead
with the beauty that comes from within,
the unfading beauty of a gentle and quiet spirit,
which is so precious to God.

1 Peter 3:4, NLT.

I Saw Jesus

Have you ever seen Jesus? I have. And I will never forget it.

It was a summer job to earn a little money for college, and I was thrilled to work at a day-care center. Eight hours a day with a dozen 4-year-olds added up to countless crafts, puppet shows, shoe-tying, and outdoor fun. One boy stood out from the rest amid all this activity.

I learned that Alan arrived first at 6:00 a.m. and left last at 6:00 p.m., only to join his single mom's night school's child care until 9:00 p.m. He was the quietest of the bunch, and usually played alone. It seemed he always wore the same clothes and was often the target of unkindness from his peers. But there was something special about Alan. He stole my heart.

With persistence, encouragement, and a little joke here and there, I worked hard at building a friendship with Alan. I believe he fully chose to trust my friendship one morning after I spent a long time combing his hair and complimenting him on his talents. I can't imagine now what we must have talked about day in and day out, but soon Alan smiled more, and he began to walk taller. Alan and I were buds. Most important, he ran and played with his friends more.

One day as I sat at the lunch table with my excited youngsters, I waited for my vegetarian plate to arrive from the cafeteria. The children were busy devouring their franks and beans. Alan sat nearest me. His hand held a forkful of hot food. Just as the fork was inches from his mouth Alan suddenly froze. Putting his fork down, he asked, "Teacher, where's your food?"

I gave a simple answer, "I don't have any lunch now." I should have explained further. Alan just sat there and watched his friends slurp up their favorite meal. He suddenly stood, picked up his little plate, stepped to my side and said, "Here, Teacher, you can have my food." And with that he gently set the plate before me.

Now I was the one who froze, overwhelmed. After catching my breath, I told Alan that my food was coming, but he chose not to eat until it arrived. How can one small boy, who had so little, give so much love—unconditionally, joyfully? And my life has never been the same. I want to allow Jesus' love to fill me so I can share as Alan did. So others can see Jesus too.

Jodie Bell Aakko

And calling to him a child, he put him in the midst of them and said, "Truly, I say to you, unless you turn and become like children, you will never enter the kingdom of heaven. Whoever humbles himself like this child is the greatest in the kingdom of heaven."
Matthew 18:2-4, ESV.

Guarding Our Children

The Messenger
of Yahweh camps
around those who
fear him, and he
rescues them.

Psalm 34:7, GW.

On a recent trip to Hawaii a girlfriend and I took the opportunity to swim with wild dolphins. We were excited, boarding the boat that would take us along the coast of Oahu. The day was beautiful; we saw the occasional whale breaching in the distance and at one point saw some large sea turtles swimming below. We were told that the dolphins are found in coves near the shore in the early morning, but later in the day they head for deeper waters to feed.

We were on one of the later trips and had been on board the boat for quite some time when our captain pointed out a distant pod of dolphins coming our way. Once the boat had us in line with their travels, we were to slip into the water with mask and snorkel, but no flippers. We were instructed to just lie there quietly while the boat maneuvered away from us. We hadn't been there long when we were literally surrounded. The dolphins were surfacing between us and diving below us. I just looked in awe at their size, beauty, and gracefulness. Despite their speed and strength, not one of them touched any of us.

We were let off the boat twice for this marvelous experience. We then headed back down the coast. We had not gone far when some of us noticed a small group of dolphins slowly circling in the water not far behind us.

When we asked the captain about them, she said that they were likely waiting for a sick or injured dolphin to join them. They would escort it safely to deeper waters. Earlier she had told us about a baby dolphin they'd seen a few days before that had been bitten by a shark and was being "guarded" by adults in a cove. Just then we saw the mom and a baby coming through the water, and watched as the other dolphins swam with them, forming a flank on either side to protect them. The baby had a distinct piece missing at the front of its dorsal fin.

The scene brought tears to my eyes. I was reminded that our loving Father not only cares for these beautiful creatures and created them with the instinct to care for one another, but that He cares for us, too, and will send legions of His angels to camp around those of us who trust Him, and when we are in need He will rescue us.

Beverly D. Hazzard

What God Loves Most Is a Beautiful Character

God is a lover of the beautiful, but that which He most loves is a beautiful character. . . . It is beauty of character that shall not perish, but last through the ceaseless ages of eternity. [1]

The great Master-Artist has taken thought for the lilies, making them so beautiful that they outshine the glory of Solomon. How much more does He care for man, who is the image and glory of God. He longs to see His children reveal a character after His similitude. As the sunbeam imparts to the flowers their varied and delicate tints, so does God impart to the soul the beauty of His own character.

All who choose Christ's kingdom of love and righteousness and peace, making its interest paramount to all other, are linked to the world above, and every blessing needed for this life is theirs. In the book of God's providence, the volume of life, we are each given a page. That page contains every particular of our history; even the hairs of the head are numbered. God's children are never absent from His mind. [2]

Worldly display, however imposing, is of no value in God's sight. Above the seen and temporal He values the unseen and eternal. The former is of worth only as it expresses the latter. The choicest productions of art possess no beauty that can compare with the beauty of character, which is the fruit of the Holy Spirit's working in the soul. . . .

Christ came to the earth and stood before the children of men with the hoarded love of eternity, and this is the treasure that, through our connection with Him, we are to receive, to reveal, and to impart. . . .

We are to be distinguished from the world because God has placed His seal upon us, because He manifests in us His own character of love. [3]

Ellen G. White

Let the beauty of the Lord our God be upon us.

Psalm 90:17.

Scars of Sacrifice

Scars are marks that last for a lifetime. I have many of them imprinted on my body—cuts, scrapes, surgeries, dog bites, and many others.

When I think about any one of my scars, almost instantly I remember the incident when it was acquired. However, if it were possible, I wouldn't have any of them, since none are on my body because of my own will. And some caused me discomfort, pain, tears, and suffering.

But . . . some scars are necessary.

A few years ago I underwent a kidney transplant. It's not a simple thing to receive an organ. The donor, in addition to being special, must be compatible with my blood and other matching characteristics. And they must be willing to donate one of their kidneys!

My sister, in an act of bravery and courage, willingly performed that sacrifice. And thanks to the grandioso love of Christ, the surgery was a success.

Today both my sister and I carry scars on our bodies. Mine reminds me that through the gesture of someone who loves me, I was liberated from spending the rest of my life on a hemodialysis machine. My sister's scar reminds her of her gesture of donation and surrender.

Christ, donor of life and liberty, offered Himself in an incomparably larger way. He did not give Himself partially, but gave Himself entirely, without reservation, showing unconditional love.

The Bible says that someone *may* give their life for a just and loving person of good character. But the fact is that Christ died for us while we were still sinners.

He gave Himself! His body is replete with scars caused by His love for both you and me. His surrender brought us life, liberating us forever from the machine of sin.

The scars upon Christ's body will prove forever the extent of His great and immeasurable love! It is my prayer that I may not only be touched by this gesture, but position myself always, confidently, and obediently, at His side. How do we say Thank You to our Father and others, such as my sister, who have done so much for us?

Jussara Alves

Reach your finger here, and look at My hands; and reach your hand here, and put it into My side.
John 20:27, NKJV.

Kindness to Others

How many things has God taught me over the years? I would say there have been hundreds. One of the most important is kindness. He has asked me to look and listen to those around me and to ask Him to show me those who need help. Is it the older woman who is crossing the street with a heavy bag? I can help her carry that bag. Sometimes I am prompted to give up my seat on the bus for a child or old man. I need to be open to God's promptings.

In college I worked very hard to pay for the college fees. Sometimes I felt that I wasn't going to get the next bill paid. I remember one Sabbath when someone asked why I wore the same two dresses to church and Sabbath school week after week. My quiet answer was "That is all I have." I felt sorry for myself even though, as always, God was already helping me. He was helping in two ways: I was learning to trust Him, and He was giving me a friend who listened to Him.

One day this girlfriend knocked on my dorm room door. When I opened the door I saw her standing there with a very big box. She seemed a little shy and that seemed strange to me, because she was a sweet and wonderful person. All of us were glad she was our friend. Quietly she asked, "Would you like the clothes in this box? I'm getting new clothes. My grandma wants to buy me some new outfits, so I don't need these. Do you want them?"

Did I! I was excited and thanked her for her gift. We hugged, and she went on her way.

Now I had more than enough clothes for the next year and beyond. More than two dresses to wear to church! This friend is still a very special person to me, and I pray that she knows what a great and kind thing she did that day.

I want to be faithful to what God asks me to do. He usually gets my attention in a clear small voice, and I pray that I do not miss helping others and seeing others with God's eyes. Another Bible version translates today's thought as this: "God's Spirit makes us loving, happy, peaceful, patient, kind, good, faithful, gentle, and self-controlled. There is no law against behaving in any of these ways. And because we belong to Christ Jesus, we have killed our selfish feelings and desires" (Galatians 5:22-24, CEV). Isn't that what we all want?

Susen Mattison Molé

We Are to Consider Nature's Lessons

Natural science is God's storehouse from which every student in the school of Christ may draw. The ways of God in natural philosophy, and the mysteries connected with His dealings with man, are a treasury from which all may draw.[4]

The flowers of the field, in their endless variety, are always ministering to the delight of the children of men. God Himself nourishes every root, that He may express His love to all who will be softened and subdued by the works of His hands. We need no artificial display. God's love is represented by the beautiful things of His creation.[5]

Christ sought to draw the attention of His disciples away from the artificial to the natural: "If God so clothe the grass of the field, which today is, and tomorrow is cast into the oven, shall he not much more clothe you, O ye of little faith!" Why did not our heavenly Father carpet the earth with brown or gray? He chose the color that was most restful, the most acceptable to the senses. How it cheers the heart and refreshes the weary spirit to look upon the earth, clad in its garments of living green! Without this covering the air would be filled with dust, and the earth would appear like a desert. Every spire of grass, every opening bud and blooming flower, is a token of God's love, and should teach us a lesson of faith and trust in Him. Christ calls our attention to their natural loveliness, and assures us that the most gorgeous array of the greatest king that ever wielded an earthly scepter was not equal to that worn by the humblest flower. You who are sighing for the artificial splendor which wealth alone can purchase, for costly paintings, furniture, and dress, listen to the voice of the divine Teacher. He points you to the flower of the field, the simple design of which cannot be equalled by human skill.[6]

Ellen G. White

And why take ye thought for raiment? Consider the lilies of the field, how they grow; they toil not, neither do they spin.
Matthew 6:28.

By Beholding
We Become Changed

I'm not a graceful person, a discovery I made as an adult when I took a class in which we exercised to music. The first couple of classes were easy enough, but soon I began to lag noticeably behind the rest of the class. I bought a CD of the music and took it home to practice in front of a mirror. That's when I made the shocking discovery that even when I succeeded in doing the motions correctly I looked like a total klutz. As much as I practiced in front of the mirror, I never learned to do the exercises gracefully.

Years later I bought an exercise DVD, but even then I had trouble making my hands and feet do the complicated motions together. Finally I learned not to look at myself but to concentrate instead on watching the teacher on the video. Amazingly, as I watched the teacher the subconscious part of my brain took over, and soon I was able to do the exercises properly. As long as I focused totally on the teacher I did well, but if I started to think about what my hands and feet were doing I became my old klutzy self.

It's a lot like that with God's grace in our spiritual lives. We can know the right things to do, and we can even do the right things; but if God's grace isn't present in our lives, even when we try to do the right things they can come out wrong. Just knowing the truth isn't enough. When God's grace is not living in us daily, even when we're right we can hurt people and turn them off—not just to us but to religion and to the gospel.

The way to become a grace-filled Christian is to concentrate on the One who is grace—Jesus. We need to spend regular, quality time beholding Him, reflecting on the One who took time to have a life-changing conversation with a woman who had had five husbands. The One who had dinner with a dishonest tax collector. The One who was humble enough to wash the feet of the very one who would betray Him.

When we concentrate on Jesus instead of on ourselves a funny thing happens. Slowly, imperceptibly, we begin to change. His will becomes our will; His thoughts become our thoughts; His ways become our ways. We become grace-filled, loving, and lovable Christians.

Carla Baker

(And we beheld his glory, the glory as of the only begotten of the Father,) full of grace and truth.

John 1:14.

Unscrambled Eggs

Before my children were born, I was second mom to several of my nieces—OK, favorite auntie. They came up to our farm. They would sleep over, and I taught them a bit about cooking and sewing. They kept my attitude more positive. Doctors had said that I would be unable to have children because of a car accident years earlier, so I enjoyed all my sisters' kids.

Once we were going to make white cakes so that each one could take a frosted layer home with white frosting, like wedding cakes, and decorate them. In her excitement Rhonnie cracked both eggs directly into the bowl and added the butter and sugar in to cream them. Billie Jean yelled, "It is supposed to be a white cake—no yolks!" Before tears could start, I assured both that the cake would be all right; it would just have a creamy white color. Once done, you cannot unscramble eggs. We enjoyed the cakes—they tasted wonderful.

Like those eggs, we cannot "unscramble" our sins. We cannot take them back. And God knows us better than anyone. We know we cannot hide our sins from Him. We can ask for forgiveness, and as praying Christians we can be assured God will forgive us. But as humans, even when we ask for someone to forgive us we can't always know whether or not the way we may have hurt them will permanently damage our relationship.

Forgiving ourselves is the hardest thing to do, but reminding God daily of sins He has thrown into the deepest seas seems redundant. It lacks the conviction of accepting His love and sacrifice. When we approach others to forgive us, we want them to see that we are repentant, that we want their forgiveness.

Most people want to forgive, but if their pain is deep they may not want to have anything to do with you for a while—or maybe never. That's when you have to move on and ask God to somehow let those folks know that we mean it and pray for them to heal. He is the only one who can unscramble our messes. In today's texts He promises to do that.

Sally J. Aken-Linke

Patience

The lives of some are without peace or gladness because they never get out of the range of self. They are ever reaching out for sympathy from others. If they would go to work to see how helpful they could be, and would speak words of love and courage, their souls, now dry and sorrowful, would become like a watered garden.

You must learn in the school of Christ precious lessons of patience. Do not become discouraged, but keep at the work in all humility. It will drive you to Jesus; it will lead you to study the Pattern. You want to work as Jesus worked.[7]

Trials will come, it is true, even to those who are fully consecrated. The patience of the most patient will be severely tested. . . . Often silence is the severest rebuke that could be given to the one who has sinned with his lips.

When they [the children and youth] lose self-control and speak words that are passionate, an attitude of silence is often the best course to pursue, not taking up a line of reproof or argument or condemnation. Repentance will come very soon. The silence that is golden will often do more than all the words that can be uttered.

When others are impatient, fretful, and complaining because self is not subdued, begin to sing some of the songs of Zion. While Christ was working at the carpenter's bench, others would sometimes surround Him, trying to cause Him to be impatient; but He would begin singing some of the beautiful psalms, and before they realized what they were doing, they had joined with Him in singing, influenced, as it were, by the power of the Holy Spirit which was there.[8]

Christ's perfect example and the grace of God are given him [man] to enable him to train his sons and daughters to be sons and daughters of God.[9]

Ellen G. White

For ye have need of patience, that, after ye have done the will of God, ye might receive the promise. Hebrews 10:36.

"Let Not Your Heart Be Troubled"

I can truthfully say that earlier in my life I did not always feel like a courageous Christian. At times I may have appeared to be a beaten-down believer. It began with the mammogram I had that spring. I was asked to return, as the doctor had viewed a suspicious mass and they felt I should undergo a biopsy. I had managed to escape the procedure a few years earlier when it was concluded a biopsy was not needed. In neither case did I feel I had total control. I leaned upon the doctors for guidance and management, just as I should have done. However, ultimately and beyond a shadow of doubt, it was clear that my all-out faith had to be in our Lord Jesus Christ. I needed His leading.

The day before the biopsy I was asked to sing at a memorial service to assist the family of a former church member with celebrating the life of their patriarch. I chose "His Eye Is on the Sparrow," by C. D. Martin, and I recall that the words really spoke to me as I sang.

When I entered the hospital the next morning, the first doctor who saw me checked my vitals. I told him that I had slept surprisingly well considering the course of the day's events. His reply was "Oh, let not your heart be troubled!" Wow! This doctor had spoken the very same scripture that was in the song. Then I realized that even in the lyrics of a song that I myself would vocalize, God would bring my worries to a standstill and help me be at peace. I just needed a "faith lift," and God used a healer to help me. And all did go fine. I am grateful for the reassurance and care from the medical personnel.

Jesus did not tell us that we should keep on worrying after praying to Him. He wants us to have faith in Him. Worrying only makes things more complicated. It is not always possible to control the circumstances in our lives, but we can be masters of our thoughts regarding what occurs. The Lord has promised to never leave us or forsake us (Hebrews 13:5). It is a matter of simple and childlike faith. Hallelujah!

Patrice Hill Taylor

"Do not be worried and upset," Jesus told them. "Believe in God and believe also in me." John 14:1, TEV.

Trusting God in All Circumstances

Trust in the Lord forever, for the Lord himself, is the Rock eternal.

Isaiah 26:4, NIV.

Several years ago I was diagnosed with Ménière's disease, an inner ear disorder that causes vertigo and hearing loss. Although Ménière's is not a life-threatening illness, it was the first time I had been faced with a health issue that couldn't be cured.

Right after I was diagnosed I looked on the Internet to find out more about the disease. When I discovered that the vertigo gets so bad in some people that they literally can't function for weeks or months at a time and that others go totally deaf in both ears, I panicked. All I could think about was that I live alone, I have to travel to earn my livelihood, and that if I lost my hearing and couldn't communicate with people I would lose my job.

One day I mentioned my fears to a small group of wise, godly women. One of them pressed me and asked, "And what would happen if you lost your job?"

"I would starve to death because I have no one to take care of me," I said.

"You aren't trusting God to take care of you," she replied, reminding me that nothing can happen to me for which God has not already made provision.

She was right. I had totally forgotten that God has always taken care of me. I had been through much tougher situations than Ménière's disease and had always felt His presence in a very real way. But I had allowed fear to rob me of the peace God intended for me. I thank the Lord for godly friends who were willing to help me confront the real issue—lack of trust. Isaiah 30:15 tells us: "In repentance and rest is your salvation, in quietness and trust is your strength" (NIV).

Quietness and trust mean not whining and asking "Why me?" when things go wrong. Paul had plenty of reason to whine and complain when he was imprisoned on trumped-up charges. Instead, he trusted God and was able to use his time productively while in prison. Some of his most encouraging Epistles to the young Christian churches were written from prison.

And by trusting in God's ability to take care of us in all circumstances, we too find the strength we need to cope with the trials that we all experience. As I have learned to trust God with my illness, He has indeed been more than faithful to enable me to do everything I need to do for my work and for living on my own.

Carla Baker

God's Plans Are Perfect

Jesus ascended to the Father as a representative of the human race, and God will bring those who reflect His image to behold and share with Him His glory. There are homes for the pilgrims of earth. There are robes for the righteous, with crowns of glory and palms of victory. All that perplexed us in the providences of God will then be made plain. The things hard to be understood will then find an explanation. The mysteries of grace will unfold before us. Where our finite minds discovered only confusion and broken purposes, we shall see the most perfect and beautiful harmony. We shall know that infinite love ordered the experiences that seemed most trying and hard to bear. As we realize the tender care of Him who makes all things work together for our good, we shall rejoice with joy unspeakable and full of glory.

Pain cannot exist in the atmosphere of heaven. In the home of the redeemed there will be no tears, no funeral trains, no badges of mourning. "The inhabitant shall not say, I am sick: the people that dwell therein shall be forgiven their iniquity" (Isaiah 33:34). One rich tide of happiness will flow and deepen as eternity rolls on. Think of this; tell it to the children of suffering and sorrow, and bid them rejoice in hope.

The nearer we come to Jesus, the more clearly we behold the purity and greatness of His character, the less we shall feel like exalting self. The contrast between our characters and His will lead to humiliation of soul and deep heart searching. The more we love Jesus, the more entirely will self be humbled and forgotten. . . .

He who is meek in spirit, he who is purest and most childlike, will be made strong for the battle. He will be strengthened with might by His Spirit in the inner man. He who feels his weakness, and wrestles with God as did Jacob, and like this servant of old cries, "I will not let thee go, except thou bless me," will go forth with the fresh anointing of the Holy Spirit. The atmosphere of heaven will surround him. He will go about doing good. His influence will be a positive force in favor of the religion of Christ. . . .

Our God is a very present help in time of need. He is acquainted with the most secret thoughts of our hearts, with all the intents and purposes of our souls. When we are in perplexity, even before we open to Him our distresses, He is making arrangements for our deliverance.[10]

> By faith he sojourned in the land of promise, as in a strange country, dwelling in tabernacles with Isaac and Jacob, the heirs with him of the same promise: for he looked for a city which hath foundations, whose builder and maker is God.
>
> Hebrews 11:9, 10.

Ellen G. White

God's Rainbow Promises

The sky was dark and foreboding as I drew near my home in the city. The clouds looked as though they would open up and drench the earth with their tears. I didn't want this darkness. I was returning from a difficult mission, and I wanted only sunshine. Though my relatives told me it was none of my business, I'd had to speak the truth to a family member who was looking for love in all the wrong places. But the Lord says that we are each other's keeper, and his life was in peril. God holds His servants accountable, and I had come too far by faith to disobey His will.

I was exhausted from the long drive back from Ohio and just wanted to get home. However, I first had to stop at the store and pick up something for dinner. Grabbing my umbrella, I dashed between downpours until I was safely inside the grocery store.

A half hour later I emerged to find that the dark clouds had disappeared, replaced by blue skies and bright sunshine. I hurriedly walked to my car and proceeded to drive home without thought or care. As I waited at a traffic light, there it was: a beautiful multihued rainbow that seemed to cover the entire city. From one spectrum to another it bowed in reverence to its Creator. Then, looking closer, I saw something I'd never experienced before—a second rainbow was tenderly cradled beneath the first. My heart was humbled, and I rejoiced at the wondrous sight. The Lord had given me a double portion of His promises!

How often we hurriedly go through life, forgetting the promises of God. How often we become consumed with the mundane things of this world, making us anxious or fearful. God's promises are real! He promises that He will be there for us during those difficult times. He promises that He will bless us, protect us, and give us His peace. He promises that if we remain faithful we will inherit His kingdom. He promises a better day, "Yes, a better day; after a while there will be a better day."

I want to remember God's promises and to keep my eyes on Him, don't you?

Evelyn Greenwade Boltwood

By which have been given to us exceedingly great and precious promises, that through these you may be partakers of the divine nature.

2 Peter 1:4, NKJV.

What Do *You* Need?

Your Father knows

what you need

before you ask.

Matthew 6:8, NIV.

Birthday dinner at Olive Garden!" chirped Melissa, looking over the menu as she had seen adults do. "This is my favorite restaurant. Let's see, what do I want?" I chuckled at her enthusiasm.

Within a minute or two a tall, slim woman stopped at our table, order pad in hand. Her eyes were red and puffy; her smile wan. Nevertheless, her voice was pleasant and well-modulated. "Hi, my name is Carianne," she said. "May I take your order?"

I turned to ask Melissa what she wanted, but her eyes were not on the menu. Instead, she was studying the woman's face. After a long moment Melissa asked the server, "What do you need?" I blinked. Where did that come from? I thought. What does she need?

The woman looked down at Melissa. "I need . . ." she began, but her voice faltered as tears chased each other down her cheeks. Carianne cleared her throat. "I need someone to visit my little girl." She explained that her 5-year-old daughter was hospitalized in a city some distance away. Once a week, on her day off, Carianne made a 12-hour round-trip to the intensive-care unit. The rest of the week there was no one to visit her child.

Melissa turned to me, menu forgotten. "We know the youth pastor in that city! Can you call her right now and ask her to make a visit?" (When Melissa gets an idea, that girl wants action.) I took out my iPhone. Within minutes, cell to cell, the youth pastor had the necessary information and was actually on her way to the hospital.

Questions tumbled out one after another from Carianne. "What made you ask that question? How can I ever thank you? What if you hadn't been seated in my section?"

Melissa's face was very serious as she replied, "I was just impressed to ask. Good thing I paid attention to my tuition." (She meant intuition.) As we worked our way through a scrumptitious meal (one of Melissa's favorite big words), I thought about her question: What do you need?

Later, as we walked out to the car, I knew what the answer was for me. Winging a prayer upward, I breathed, "I need You in my life—always." What do you need? If you aren't sure, God can help you figure it out.

Arlene R. Taylor

The Smiles of God

Nothing can do us real good without the blessing of God. What God blesses is blessed. Therefore "a little that a righteous man hath is better than the riches of many wicked." Psalm 37:16. The little with the blessing of God is more efficient, and it will extend farther. The grace of God will make a little go a great ways. When we devote ourselves to the affairs of the kingdom of God, He will mind our affairs."[11]

The Lord has given us precious blessings in the simple flowers of the field, in the fragrance so grateful to our senses. He has tinted every flower with beauty; for He is the great Master Artist. He who has created the beautiful things in nature will do far greater things for the soul. God is a lover of the beautiful, and He would adorn our characters with His own rich graces. He would have our words as fragrant as the flowers of the field. He has given us blessings in daily provision for our physical needs. The very bread we eat has upon it the image and superscription of the cross.[12]

They only are truly blessed whose chief concern is to secure those blessings which will nourish the soul and endure forever. Our Savior says to us, "Seek ye first the kingdom of God, and his righteousness; and all these things shall be added unto you." Matthew 6:33. God has a care for us, even to bestow His temporal blessings upon us. Our earthly good is not beneath the notice of our heavenly Father. He knoweth that we have need of these things. . . . When God smiles upon our efforts it is worth more than any earthly income.

"How sweet our daily comforts prove
 When they are seasoned with His love."[13]

Every deliverance, every blessing, that God in the past has granted to His people should be kept fresh in memory's hall as a sure pledge of further and richer, increasing blessings that He will bestow.[14]

There is no limit to the blessings that it is our privilege to receive.[15]

Ellen G. White

The blessing of the Lord, it maketh rich, and he addeth no sorrow with it.

Proverbs 10:22.

Leaning on God

In Pisa's Cathedral Square stands a bell tower called the Leaning Tower of Pisa. It started to sink shortly after construction began, causing it to lean increasingly over the years. The tower has some parallels to my life.

I see an increasing tilt in my spiritual experience over the years that corresponds to times I sank with the vicissitudes of life and leaned more on the Lord. I was baptized in 1959, but I think at that time (and for years afterward) I leaned on my grandmother more than I leaned on the Lord. My grandmother would rise before daybreak, kneel by her bed, and audibly talk to the Lord. She prayed for the country, the government, friends and family whom she called by name. I remember being thrilled each time I heard my name. Her prayers on my behalf were so comprehensive they made mine seem redundant. She made me feel safe and blessed. When she went to sleep in Jesus while I was in medical school, I was devastated. I didn't think then that I could survive without her intercessory prayers, and surely I would never be successful in my final examinations, as she had prayed me through every examination that I had sat for to that date. That's when I really started to lean—but this time on the Lord.

Over the years I've had what seems to be more than my fair share of disappointments and challenges related to my job, family, health, retirement, and events that I file under miscellaneous. I've experienced sorrow as I watched close friends suffer and die. With each event I have tilted more, as I leaned more on the Lord, who not only has been my greatest source of support but also has blessed me with great friends who provide earthly support.

My angle of tilt continues to increase, and I'm now close to horizontal. This has placed me in a wonderful position to look more upward, and I am amazed by the big picture of my life—a fulfilled life, totally ordered by God. I've seen disappointments turn out for my good. Most of my goals now have been achieved. All my need, and some of my wants, have been supplied. I enjoy better health than many, and I now see each past trial as a learning experience that tilted me one degree closer to the Lord. I feel blessed and totally protected in His arms.

Cecelia Grant

The Lord is my rock, and my fortress, and my deliverer, my God, my rock, in whom I take refuge, my shield, and the horn of my salvation, my stronghold.

Psalm 18:2, RSV.

Welcome Home!

Father, I want those
you have given
me to be with me
where I am, and to
see my glory, the
glory you have given
me because you
loved me before the
creation of the world.

John 17:24, NIV.

In the greatest homecoming of all time, the resurrected Jesus returns to His heavenly home escorted by an eager, shining cloud of angels. All heaven is waiting to welcome the Savior back to the celestial courts.

As the entourage nears the city, the escorting angels shout out a challenge to the sentinel angels waiting at heaven's gate. "Lift up your heads, you gates; be lifted up, you ancient doors, that the King of glory may come in."

The sentinel angels respond: "Who is this King of glory?" then wait in breathless anticipation for the answer they already know.

"The Lord strong and mighty, the Lord mighty in battle," the escorting angels shout joyously. "Lift up your heads, you gates; lift them up, you ancient doors, that the King of glory may come in," they demand in delight.

Again comes the challenge from the sentinel angels: "Who is he, this King of glory?" (for they never tire of hearing His name exalted).

"The Lord Almighty—he is the King of glory," shout the escorting angels (Psalm 24:7-10, NIV).

The angelic throng sweeps through heaven's wide-open gates, voices soaring in rapturous music. The Son, the beloved Son, has come home! Past the assembled sons of God and the heavenly council He strides, straight to His Father's encircling arms.

"Justice is satisfied!" His Father declares.

Love has conquered. The lost is found. Once more the family of heaven and the family of earth are one.

There will be another homecoming soon, a most glorious homecoming, a victory celebration of the love relationship that already exists between the One who is coming and those who wait for Him.

"I'm coming, My little ones," Jesus promises, "coming to bring you home to My Father!"

Jeannette Busby Johnson

Changes Our Constant Complaining to Praise

We are heaven-bound, and we should show the attractive part of our faith. We should not go as a crippled band of mourners, groaning and complaining all along the journey to our Father's house.[16]

Those professed Christians who are constantly complaining, who seem to think happiness and a cheerful countenance a sin, have not the genuine attributes of religion. Those who look upon nature's beautiful scenery as they would upon a dead picture; who choose to look upon dead leaves rather than to gather the beautiful flowers; who take a mournful pleasure in all that is melancholy in the language spoken to them by the natural world; who see no beauty in valleys clothed in living green, and grand mountain heights clothed with verdure; who close their senses to the joyful voice that speaks to them in nature . . .—these are not in Christ.[17]

Suppose we change this order of things. . . . Suppose you try to count all your blessings. You have thought so little upon them, and they have been so continual, that when reverses or afflictions come, you are grieved, and think God is unjust. You do not call to mind how little gratitude you have manifested for all the blessings of God. You have not deserved them; but because they have flowed in upon you day by day, year by year, you have looked upon them as a matter of course, thinking it was your right to receive every advantage, and give nothing in return. . . . The blessings of God are more than the hairs of our head, more than the sands of the seashore. Meditate upon His love and care for us, and may it inspire you with love that trials cannot interrupt nor afflictions quench.[18]

If we could only see the many dangers from which we are daily preserved by the holy angels, instead of complaining of our trials and misfortunes, we would talk continually of the mercies of God.[19]

Ellen G. White

O that men would praise the Lord for his goodness, and for his wonderful works to the children of men! Psalm 107:8.

Good News!

I waited for Mary, the bank teller that I wanted, for Mary was the mother of one of my son's schoolmates. Her face beamed when she recognized me, and she happily announced, "We have a diagnosis for John! He has cerebral palsy!"

I responded happily to her joy, "Oh, how wonderful!"

Immediately I heard the gasp of those in line behind me. They pulled back, horrified at the exchange they had just overheard. Not knowing the circumstances behind my joy at hearing that a friend's son had cerebral palsy, they judged my response as inappropriate.

It is so easy to judge others by our knowledge and experience without knowing the circumstances behind the situation. These were the circumstances in this case. Less than a week after his birth, John became very jaundiced. When the jaundice was eliminated, the illness left him totally unable to move his arms and legs or to make a sound. For the six years before I met them, Mary and her husband had taken John to an array of specialists, desperately trying to find out what was wrong. Without a diagnosis, nothing could be done to help their child.

I had met Mary and John four years earlier when, at age 6, John joined my son's class in a school for those with disabilities. He came in a wheelchair, unable to move his arms or legs. But John's eyes were bright, aware, and alert, full of fun and intelligence. He followed what happened around him and paid close attention in his classes.

Now, four years later, the search for a diagnosis had finally been successful. Mary was bubbling with joy and hope as she continued talking to me, totally unaware of the horrified responses of those around us. "They tell me he will talk by age 12, walk by 16, and probably be able to graduate with his class at 18. Oh, Darlene, now that they have a diagnosis, they know how to treat him, and my John can have a life!"

We dare not judge others by what we think we know as their life walk is different from ours, and only God knows their situation. May He give us wisdom and discernment!

Darlenejoan McKibbin Rhine

Judge not. . . .
Why beholdest thou
the mote that is in thy
brother's eye,
but considerest not
the beam that is in
thine own eye?

Matthew 7:1-3.

Miracles for Our Children

I will fight those who fight you, and I will save your children.

Isaiah 49:25, NLT.

Perhaps you've experienced the pain of seeing a child "crash" in one way or another. A horrified mother once watched her 19-year-old crash into an ice rink wall as he was practicing for a skating competition. J. R. Celski lay on the ice, blood pouring from the gaping wound his skate blade had made when it sliced across his left thigh.

Because my children have taken an occasional nasty spill on life's skating rink, I took special notice when this young man won his first Olympic medal just months later because he really shouldn't have been there. But then again, he had a mother rooting for him!

Amazingly, Celski managed to compete in the Vancouver Olympics 1,500-meter short-track speed skating final. He held a dismal fifth-place position on the last turn. Television cameras briefly panned to the stands to his mother's tense face as she cheered him on.

Suddenly, for no apparent reason, the skaters in the silver and bronze positions crashed, and young J. R. Celski whizzed across the finish line in third place—an Olympic medalist! "Kind of a miracle" is how one sports reporter described the skater's unexpected finish.

The Originator of miracles is still working in response to mothers' prayers—especially when it comes to bringing their children across heaven's finish line. No matter how badly our kids crash, we can still cheer them on by claiming promises of blessing as in today's text.

For years a friend of mine, whom I'll call Sonny, crashed repeatedly— morally, physically, spiritually. Until the moment of her death, however, Sonny's mother claimed promises for her son's salvation. Years later Sonny met and accepted Jesus Christ as Lord of his life. That's kind of a miracle too, isn't it!

Sonny likes to describe what the next reunion with his mother will be like. He says, "When I cross that finish line stretched between heaven's pearly gates, my mother will see me. Her first words will be 'Praise God, Sonny— how on earth did you get here?'" And my response will be "By the grace of God, Mama, and because of your prayers of faith."

Let's fight for all our kids on our knees before God's open Word. Let's cheer them on when they're doing their best. And finally, let's trust God to work His last-minute miracles in their lives.

Carolyn Sutton

The Holy Spirit
Our Helper

Through the ministry of the angels the Holy Spirit is enabled to work upon the mind and heart of the human agent and draw him to Christ. . . . But the Spirit of God does not interfere with the freedom of the human agent. The Holy Spirit is given to be a helper, so that man may cooperate with the Divine, and it is given to Him to draw the soul but never to force obedience.

Christ is ready to impart all heavenly influences. He knows every temptation that comes to man, and the capabilities of each. He weighs his strength. He sees the present and the future, and presents before the mind the obligations that should be met, and urges that common, earthly things shall not be permitted to be so absorbing that eternal things shall be lost out of the reckoning. The Lord has fullness of grace to bestow on every one that will receive of the heavenly gift. The Holy Spirit will bring the God-entrusted capabilities into Christ's service, and will mold and fashion the human agent according to the divine Pattern.[20]

The Holy Spirit is our efficiency in the work of character building, in forming characters after the divine similitude. When we think ourselves capable of molding our own experience, we make a great mistake. We can never of ourselves obtain the victory over temptation. But those who have genuine faith in Christ will be worked by the Holy Spirit. The soul in whose heart faith abides will grow into a beautiful temple for the Lord. He is directed by the grace of Christ. Just in proportion as he depends on the Holy Spirit's teaching he will grow.[21]

The influence of the Holy Spirit is the life of Christ in the soul. We do not now see Christ and speak to Him, but His Holy Spirit is just as near us in one place as another. It works in and through every one who receives Christ. Those who know the indwelling of the Spirit reveal the fruit of the Spirit— love, joy, peace, long-suffering, gentleness, goodness, faith.[22]

Ellen G. White

For as many as are led by the Spirit of God, they are the sons of God.

Romans 8:14.

Taking Care of *All* Our Needs

My husband and I were planning a pleasure trip and trying to decide the best way to travel. Should we go by train, with an eight-hour layover, by plane, which was very expensive, or by bus, which would take a long 18 hours. We prayed and discussed it. Because my husband is legally sightless, the ultimate decision was his to make. A few days passed and he announced, "We should take the bus, and I'll be able to 'see' some of the countryside." We chose a schedule, and I started packing.

During a two-hour wait at the bus terminal I picked up our tickets and began observing my surroundings. I noticed a young man sitting with three other people. After a while I saw him escort a young man who appeared to be mentally challenged to the restroom. As we began boarding, he was in front of us and we exchanged a few pleasantries. We sat in our priority seats, and he sat almost across from us. At our second stop my husband wanted to use the restroom. I thought, *Lord, how should I do this? I don't want him going in there by himself, and I can't go in there with him.* Then I saw the same young man coming out of the door. He acknowledged us, and in that instant something said to me, "Ask him."

I said, *No, he doesn't know us!* Then I heard again, "Ask him!" so I called out to him, "Excuse me, sir, could you please do me a favor?"

He said, "Sure!" I asked if he would escort my husband to the restroom. He nodded yes, and took my husband's arm. My husband quickly asked, "Sir, who are you?"

"My name is Charles," he said, "and I'm going to escort you to the restroom."

From then on whenever we made a stop, Charles came and checked with my husband to see if he needed anything. He heard him say he was cold so he asked the driver to turn down the air. Charles was from our hometown, and he had attended the same high school as our children.

When we arrived at our destination, Charles made sure we retrieved our luggage and that someone was there to meet us. Now I know our trip had been carefully preplanned. Our angel was there waiting on us. God said He would take care of all our needs.

> Be not forgetful to entertain strangers: for thereby some have entertained angels unawares.
> Hebrews 13:2.

Elaine J. Johnson

I Need a Good Sharp Knife

For months I'd been shopping for a good sharp knife. I had so many knives in my drawer, but they were all blunt. My search for a good knife began when a friend invited us for a weekend. I volunteered to prepare the salad, and as I chopped the parsley the knife just went very smoothly, no effort needed. "Wow!" I exclaimed. "This is a good knife!"

I bought several knives after that, but I wasn't satisfied. They weren't sharp like my friend's knife, and not sharp enough for my salads.

One day as I helped a friend in her kitchen, I noticed that before she used the knife she had a long iron-looking thing she called a sharpener that she used to sharpen the knife. I asked if I could try it, and after using it, I was amazed. It worked! The knife became so sharp!

The next day at home I decided to try it. I don't have a sharpener, so I used another knife on my favorite knife. And it worked! I couldn't believe how sharp my knife became. My searching was over. I have all the knives I need—all I have to do is sharpen them.

As I contemplated this, two things came to mind: First, we have all that we really need to be good, sharp Christians: Christians whom people would like to have around, Christians who lead people to exclaim, "This is good!" Yes, we have everything within our reach and at our call. Our Bibles are there to guide us and to sharpen our faith. God is just a prayer away from us; He is the one who can make us good and sharp.

Second, it tells me that we are God's knives, His tools to penetrate into the hearts of people. But before He can use us effectively He first sharpens us that we may be knowledgeable about His will for us and His people. So as we go through the "sharpening" process, as we go through hardship and trials in life, know that we are being sharpened for His service. Only after the sharpening do we become polished, loving, and lovable Christians.

Jemima Dollosa Orillosa

Life of Cheerful Submission

Jesus claimed His sonship to the Eternal. . . . His first visit to the temple had awakened new impulses. All earthly obligations were, for the time, lost sight of; but with the knowledge of His divine mission, and of His union with God, He did not resist the authority of His parents. At their request He returned with them as a faithful, obedient son, and aided them in their life of toil. He buried in His own heart the secret of His future mission, waiting submissively until the period of His public ministry should commence before announcing to the world that He was the Messiah. He submitted to parental restraint, for the period of eighteen years after He had acknowledged that He was the Son of God, and lived the simple, common life of a Galilean, working at the carpenter's trade. . . . For thirty years He submitted to parental restraint. . . .

It is common for children, even of Christian parents, when not over twelve years old, to feel that they must be allowed to follow their own desires. And parents are ready to be led by their children, rather than to lead them. . . . For this reason many youth come up with habits of selfishness and idleness. They are vain, proud, and headstrong.[23]

When we look upon His patient self-denial, His shrinking from all notoriety, devoting Himself to His daily labor in a humble sphere, what a beautiful light is shed about His life! How clearly is pointed out the path in which children and youth should walk! . . . Jesus was no less the Son of God in His lowly home, in His submission to His parents, than when God spoke from His eternal throne, saying, "This is my beloved Son."[24]

The life of Christ assures a blessing forever upon a life of cheerful submission to parental restraint and a life of physical and mental industry.[25]

Ellen G. White

And he went down with them, and came to Nazareth, and was subject unto them.

Luke 2:51.

The Gift of Life

My husband and I are the proud parents of two girls. Shortly after our second daughter, Shelley, was born, we learned that she had cystic fibrosis. Nevertheless, Shelley lived through her childhood and early adulthood as a healthy, active, happy child. But at the age of 24, one year after she was married, she became very ill with a flu virus that collapsed both lungs, leaving her with only 17 percent lung capacity. The doctors then felt that it was the time for a lung transplant, and she was placed on the transplant list.

After a few months it was realized that cadaver lungs couldn't be obtained in time, and the doctors suggested that she have a live donor transplant. Feeling that this was the answer to our prayers, all of the family and her husband were tested to type our blood. To our dismay, all of us had different blood types than Shelley. We thought that her chances were gone.

As we discussed our situation, our other son-in-law said, "I have her blood type: I'll donate." Tears rose in my eyes as I said, "Darin, do you realize what this means?"

"Of course," he stated. "But she's my sister."

A second donor was needed. News quickly spread of our need, and 29 others were tested. After extensive testing a donor was found: Kevin, a friend Shelley had played softball with.

The day finally came, and as I stood in the pre-op area, I looked over the three gurneys that held three people I loved very much. All three would be in surgery at the same time; two would be the givers, and one the receiver. Each of the three had the chance of not making it through surgery. It was then that today's text ran through my mind. I loved my daughter so much that there wasn't anything I wouldn't do to save her. These two men who were prepared to give a part of their bodies also loved her. I wondered, how many people would do this?

I then thought about our heavenly Father and how much He loved His Son Jesus, and of the decision that they made. This world is full of people who are selfish and self-absorbed; most would deny His gift of love and tender mercy to them. But to the few who would accept Him, He gave His life so that they could escape Satan's hold and could go to live with Him forever. For the few, He told His Father, "I will go; I am the only one who can pay their price."

Greater love hath no man than this, that a man lay down his life for his friends. John 15:13.

Pamela McPherson Ross

Sometimes You Just Gotta Laugh

A merry heart does good, like medicine.

Proverbs 17:22, NKJV.

It had been a dismal week—no, a dismal month, and more. Not that anything really awful was going on. No illness. No money problems, other than never having a cent left over for extras. Simply the usual bits of life—working, cooking, cleaning, washing . . . and there was never, ever enough time.

So when Noelle had a fever that morning and didn't feel like going to church, I was glad to stay home and let the others go without us. I was too tired to go anyway. Or maybe I was more weary than tired. At any rate, I was happy to forgo pantyhose for my comfortable old robe. For a few hours it would be just me and our 10-year-old daughter. We'd have a quiet, relaxing morning.

First there was orange juice and cereal; then we decided to play Bible charades. I sat comfortably on the floor, resting against the wall, and let Noelle go first.

She stood before me in jeans and T-shirt, her pale-gold hair in thick braids. Hands at her sides, she jumped straight up, then came down. Up. Down. Up. Down. *What is she doing?* A smile lit her eyes. "Mommy, guess!" she commanded, but my mind was blank. She did it again. A smile filling her face, she raised herself on her tiptoes, then went down. Up. Down. Up. Down. For variation, a little jump up, then back down.

"Old or New Testament?" I asked.

Up . . . down . . . up . . . down. "Old."

This went on for a few minutes, with brief stops for Noelle to giggle and for me to laugh. I had no idea what she was doing, what Bible scene she was reenacting. "Give me a hint," I begged.

"It has to do with Daniel," she said. Up. Down. Up. Down.

"I give up!" I said at last.

"Are you sure?"

"Yes, I'm sure."

"I'm one of the teeth in the lion's mouth that couldn't eat Daniel!"

I started giggling, then laughing. Soon I was doubled over with laughter as I pulled my little girl down on my lap. We sat there together, laughing until our sides hurt. Laughing until I felt neither tired nor weary nor depressed. Laughing until my heart sang!

Sometimes, what you need most of all—is to laugh.

Penny Estes Wheeler

The Beauty of Nature

The childhood and youth of Christ were spent in humble circumstances, under conditions that were favorable to the development of a sound constitution. His life was passed mostly in the open air. He drank of the pure streams of water, and ate the fruit of the gardens. He passed up and down the steep mountain paths, and through the streets of Nazareth, as He went to and from His place of toil to His home. He enjoyed the varied notes of the birds as they caroled forth their praise to their Creator. He took delight in the beauty of the flowers that decked the fields. He noted with joy the glory of the heavens, the splendor of sun, moon, and stars, and looked upon the rising and setting sun with admiration. The book of nature was open before Him, and He enjoyed its tender lessons. The everlasting hills, the olive groves, were favorite places of resort where He went to commune with His Father. He was filled with divine wisdom, and through the study of nature, and by meditation upon and communion with God, His spiritual powers were strengthened.[26]

The Redeemer of the world passed up and down the hills and mountains, from the great plain to the mountain valley. He enjoyed nature's beautiful scenery. He was delighted with the fields glowing with the beautiful flowers, and in listening to the birds of the air, and uniting His voice with them in their happy songs of praise.[27]

In the life of Christ, His childhood and youth, there is a lesson for the youth of today. Christ is our example, and in youth we should contemplate God in nature—study His character in the work of His hands. The mind is strengthened by becoming acquainted with God, by reading His attributes in the things which He has made. As we behold the beauty and grandeur in the works of nature, our affections go out after God; and . . . our souls are invigorated by coming in contact with the Infinite through His marvelous works.[28]

Ellen G. White

Speak to the earth, and it shall teach thee.

Job 12:8.

You Have Granted Her Heart's Desire

Many times throughout my life God's presence has been very real to me. I have been blessed in the physical realm to know that God was near. One time in particular stands out to me more than the rest.

It was right before Thanksgiving, and my husband and I were attending Andrews University. As most students who are working their way through school, we didn't have a lot of money, and that fall we had many needs. We had invited my mom and stepdad to Thanksgiving dinner along with numerous students who didn't have funds to get home for the holiday.

During a quiet moment in my tiny kitchen I had some alone-time with God. I was thinking how nice it would be to have matching dishes for our dinner. Also, at this time, our youngest daughter had outgrown her shoes, and we couldn't afford to buy new ones. I was thinking, *God, it surely would be nice to have matching dishes and some shoes for our girl*. No more than a thought. These desires were not voiced to anyone. Merely a mother's heart echoed in her mind.

The next morning when I went outside on the porch I saw a box. Not knowing who had put it there or what was inside, I was excited to open it. Being a poor college student brings excitement over things like that. So I brought the box inside our 750-square-foot house and began to open it. It held a plastic bag that I couldn't see through and something beneath that. Underneath the bag was a set of matching dishes! They weren't brand-new, but it was a full eight-piece set with all the trimmings! My throat began to tighten. I opened the bag. To my great joy I found six pairs of shoes that just fit our little girl!

As tears rolled down my face, I whispered, *God! How? How can You love me this much? I didn't even say it out loud. It was just a thought!*

There He was. Larger than life. My God. My King. In a box of dishes and a bag of little girl's shoes. My heart soared, knowing that the King of the universe had just sat with me as I opened a cardboard box full of His love.

Tanya Kennedy

> You have granted [her] heart's desire and have not withheld the request of [her] lips.
>
> Psalm 21:2, NIV.

Your Driver Today Is . . .

I will instruct you and
teach you in the way
you should go;
I will counsel you with
my loving eye on you.

Psalm 32:8, NIV.

I felt anxious and stressed as I stepped onto the shuttle bus that ran from the long-term airport parking lot to the terminal. It was still early in the morning, but I'd been up a couple hours putting last-minute items in my suitcase, getting my water bottle filled—well, you know how it is just before you leave on a trip. As usual, I wished I had at least another day to get everything ready to leave home. I had driven the hour to the airport, parked the car, and gotten my suitcase, carry-on bag, purse, and papers gathered up and transferred. What had I forgotten? Would the security lines be as bad as they'd been last time? Would I have time to get something to eat before I needed to board my flight? So many concerns!

But now I settled into my seat on the shuttle and looked around. And then I saw it. There, above the windshield, was a small sign that read: "Your driver today is: Jesus."

I smiled, took a deep breath, and relaxed. Jesus was my driver. I didn't need to be stressed anymore. Now, I know that Jesus is a common Hispanic name, and the sign really had nothing to do with my Lord and Redeemer. However, it did remind me that if I let Jesus, my God, be my driver, be in control of my day and my life, I could relax. My blood pressure could return to normal, and I could enjoy my day. When I let Jesus take control, I can know that what happens is something that God wants, or allows, to happen.

I find this promise of how it can work so reassuring: "May the God of peace, . . . that great Shepherd of the sheep, equip you with everything good for doing his will, and may he work in us what is pleasing to him, through Jesus Christ, to whom be glory for ever and ever. Amen" (Hebrews 13:20, 21, NIV).

How about you? Is Jesus your driver today? It is so important that I allow Jesus to be my driver. Not only must I let Him be my driver—I must also let Him pick the destination and how I will get there. Handing over control can be so hard, but so rewarding!

I think it is time for me to move out of the driver's seat and let Jesus take over permanently—and no backseat driving!

Ardis Dick Stenbakken

We Are to Be
Holy as Christ Is Holy

With our limited powers we are to be as holy in our sphere as God is holy in His sphere.[29]

God expects us to build characters in accordance with the Pattern set before us. We are to lay brick upon brick, adding grace to grace, finding our weak points and correcting them in accordance with the directions given. When a crack is seen in the walls of a mansion, we know that something about the building is wrong. In our character building, cracks are often seen. Unless these defects are remedied, the house will fall when the tempest of trial beats upon it.

God gives us strength, reasoning power, time, in order that we may build characters on which He can place His stamp of approval. He desires each child of His to build a noble character, by the doing of pure, noble deeds, that in the end He may present a symmetrical structure, a fair temple, honored by man and God.

In our character building we must build on Christ. He is the sure foundation—a foundation which can never be moved. The tempest of temptation and trial cannot move the building which is riveted to the Eternal Rock. He who would grow into a beautiful building for the Lord must cultivate every power of the being. It is only by the right use of the talents that the character can develop harmoniously. Thus we bring to the foundation that which is represented in the Word as gold, silver, precious stones—material that will stand the test of God's purifying fires.[30]

Holiness is . . . an entire surrender of the will to God; it is living by every word that proceeds from the mouth of God; it is doing the will of our heavenly Father; it is trusting God in trial, in darkness as well as in light; it is walking by faith and not by sight; it is relying on God with unquestioning confidence, and resting in His love.[31]

Ellen G. White

Be ye holy;

for I am holy.

1 Peter 1:16.

Blooms of Love

For many days during a recent spring and summer my heart had been sorrowful as I'd mourned the loss of my brother and sister-in-law. In mid-February they and fellow passengers had disappeared in the Venezuelan jungle when the mission airplane my brother, Bob Norton, piloted went down. Weeks of searching had turned into months as summer lengthened toward autumn, and still nothing. My heart had often been heavy with grief and lack of answers. I couldn't understand how any good could come from such a tragic loss. Now the indigenous people served by the airplane had no one to come for their sick and wounded. My tears had been for their loss as well as my own.

One morning as I watered the ivy we grow in our greenhouses I noticed my special azalea plant still had blooms. As I gazed at the red flowers I recalled that the first flowers had appeared in February, and it had been blooming ever since. Usually my bush blooms two, or possibly three, times a year, but never continually. Jesus whispered, "These blossoms are from Me. They are to remind you of life. In this season when you mourn, these blooms are My gift to you."

It is September now, and my bush continues setting buds. The lovely blooms are a constant reminder to me of the eternal life I will share with my dear ones who love Jesus. Although what happened to the airplane and passengers remains a mystery, I have the assurance of being reunited with Bob and Neiba when Jesus returns.

In this sinful world tragedies occur. Death rips loved ones from us. Sorrow is our lot. We have more questions than answers. There is silence and darkness. But friend, I can testify that in the midst of suffering and pain, God is there. During my difficult experience I have clung to His promise "I will never leave you nor forsake you" (Joshua 1:5, NIV). I have cried out to my heavenly Father, and He has whispered messages of love and comfort to my aching heart.

Today I pulled off the dried, dead blooms from my azalea bush and marveled at the tiny buds still forming on its twigs. Jesus' message is clear: "I am the resurrection and the life. The one who believes in me will live, even though they die" (John 11:25, NIV).

He will swallow up death in victory; and the Lord God will wipe away tears from off all faces; and the rebuke of his people shall he take away from off all the earth: for the Lord hath spoken it.

Isaiah 25:8.

Barbara Ann Kay

Familiar Family Traits

So God created mankind in his own image, in the image of God he created them; male and female he created them.

Genesis 1:27, NIV.

"Does she have crooked pinkies?" I asked my oldest son, Greg, a few hours after his wife delivered their first child. I could hardly wait for his answer. We had talked many times before about our family trait—crooked pinkies—and chuckled about how people had reacted to them over the years. Maybe Avery had crooked pinkies too.

"I don't know, Ma," he answered. "Her hands are so tiny, I was afraid to touch them. But she's got big dimples, like me." As I held the phone and heard more about my newest little granddaughter, I could picture Greg's deep dimples and his winning smile.

The next day Greg called again. "Yep, she has my crooked pinkies," he said proudly.

I saw them for myself a few days later. How cute they were, and so curved. One curved considerably more than the other, just like Greg's fingers, and just like mine. I immediately thought back to Greg's birth and how I discovered his pinkies as I held him a few hours after he was born. And now Avery, a beautiful baby created in the image of her father, grandmother, great-grandfather, and many other ancestors who had perhaps inherited them too. I was ecstatic knowing my newest granddaughter had the family trait, even though Greg had told me a year before that he had researched crooked pinkies and found out that it was a birth defect, a minor congenital malformation caused by underdevelopment of the middle bone in the finger. It was called clinodactyly, curving of the little finger toward the ring finger.

How ecstatic God must have been—creating man and woman in His own image—knowing that they would be like Him in mind and character, His perfect creations. And how sad when the beauty of His handiwork was marred by sin, and the resulting evil passed down to every generation since—God's characteristics masked by wicked thoughts, words, and actions. I see it every day in the attitudes of my three older granddaughters whose sweet and adorable innocence is being replaced with mean-spirited behavior. I see it in my own unChristlike attitude and deeds as I encounter work colleagues, grocery store clerks, or unkind neighbors. I see it in church members who profess the love of God and greet each other with a hug but turn away to gossip or stir up controversy. God's family traits, part of our DNA, are missing.

Iris L. Kitching

Learning of God Through His Works

We love to contemplate the character and love of God in His created works. What evidences has He given the children of men of His power, as well as of His parental love! He has garnished the heavens and made grand and beautiful the earth.

"O Lord our Lord, how excellent is thy name in all the earth! . . . When I consider thy heavens, the work of thy fingers, the moon and the stars, which thou hast ordained; what is man, that thou art mindful of him? and the son of man, that thou visitest him?" "All thy works praise thee, O Lord; and thy saints shall bless thee" (Psalm 8:1-4; 145:10).

Had our world been formed with a perfectly level surface the monotony would have fatigued the eye and wearied the senses. God has adorned our world with grand mountains, hills, valleys, and ranges of mountains. The rugged granite, bare mountains, also the mountains decorated with evergreens and verdure, and the valleys with their softened beauty make the world a mirror of loveliness. The goodness, wisdom, and power of God are manifest everywhere. In mountains, rocks, hills, and valleys, I see the works of divine power. I can never be lonely while viewing the grand scenery of nature. On the journey over the plains and mountains I have had feelings of the deepest reverence and awe while viewing the frowning precipice and snow-capped mountain heights.

The mountains, hills, and valleys should be to us as schools in which to study the character of God in His created works. The works of God which we may view in the ever-varying scenes—in mountains, hills, and valleys, in trees, shrubs, and flowers, in every leaf, every spire of grass—should teach us lessons of the skill and love of God and of His infinite power.

Those who study nature cannot be lonesome. They love the quiet hours of meditation, for they feel that they are brought in close communion with God while tracing His power in His created works.[32]

Ellen G. White

The Lord is good to all: and his tender mercies are over all his works.
All thy works shall praise thee, O Lord; and thy saints shall bless thee.
Psalm 145:9, 10.

Pray Without Ceasing

At the time of this writing I am two weeks from having found out that I have an unhealthy breast lump. After further testing it's been determined to be malignant.

Now let me tell you, in an instant I got a greater and clearer understanding of what "pray without ceasing" means. I now have a greater sense of what "lean on Me" and "in everything give thanks" means. You see, I am a go-get-'em type of woman. Yet on this occasion I heard, "Be still and know that I am God." I heard, "Wait, I have a plan."

Let me share. You women who have experienced a mammogram machine might get a laugh (obviously, a man designed that machine). I had avoided it, but this time it was unavoidable. Actually, that process wasn't too bad. Yep, I know: in all things give thanks. It was when I went from the mammogram to the biopsy, where they take out core cells to check, that I was sweating—perspiration wall-to-wall. My blood pressure went up, although I was humming hymns out loud and tears were filling my eyes. And this was all before they even started.

Now, I was praying up a storm. In fact, I was praying up a tornado. And then it was that I heard, "Praise Me!" So there I was, lying on my side, one naked breast pointing out into the world for all to see, and I asked, "Can I put my iPod in?"

"Yes," they agreed. I sang at the top of my voice. Only the doctor and nurse and heaven heard, but I felt nothing but the love of God as they taped me up, and off I went.

I found myself trawling through all the information people have sent me and wondering how I would know what God wanted me to do. Then I remembered that every time I have asked for God's leading, He has led. So why not ask Him now? So for everything that has come across my path, I have asked God if He wants me to do this at this time. And I appreciate that I have had yes or no answers very quickly.

Why am I sharing this story? Because God is the God of love—yep, God is love. My learning has been that I was praying so feverishly that I wasn't being quiet so as to hear from my God. Once I listened, I heard. When I heard, I had peace. Healing is in His hand: physical, emotional, and spiritual.

Julie Nagle

Rejoice always, pray without ceasing, in everything give thanks; for this is the will of God in Christ Jesus for you.

1 Thessalonians. 5:16-18, NKJV.

I Will Be With You

When you pass

through the waters

I will be with you;

and through the

rivers, they shall not

overwhelm you;

when you walk

through fire you shall

not be burned, and

the flame shall not

consume you.

Isaiah 43:2, RSV.

At twilight on a fall day my parents, Marvin and Emma Dick, realized that the storms up the creek were about to cause a flash flood in the creek near their home. The cattle grazing nearby were in danger, so they both rushed out to cut the fence wires to allow their cattle to escape.

The waters rose dangerously fast. Marvin, ahead of Emma, realized immediate peril and yelled for her to go back. The flood's roar caused misunderstanding, and she thought he told her to come closer. Just seconds later the waters became too swift. He climbed a nearby tree, but she hadn't yet reached the woods. Swift water swept her off her feet, and the only thing to grab was the top fence wire. Marvin watched her floating until darkness obscured his view. Sometimes Marvin saw her flashlight beam, but his heart sank when he saw a light go bobbing down the creek. Until morning he didn't know if she'd dropped the flashlight or been swept away.

Hours passed as cold, wet tiredness took over, and Emma could no longer hang on to the meager fence wire. Her hands let go, or maybe the wire broke. Wet winter garments would have made swimming difficult, but in this overpowering current it was impossible.

Prayer had already been a major part of this whole experience. Emma floated above and under water, while her prayer thoughts turned to Isaiah, today's text. Even though she had no power, panic did not control her because she knew God's capabilities. Against circling, strong currents, angels must have helped her climb into an Osage orange tree (a thorn tree), where she spent the rest of the night.

The next morning Duke's barking alerted neighbors to my parents' problem. They brought a fishing boat and saved them both. Because of wounds from the thorns, it took Emma weeks before she could button her own buttons. But she went through the raging water and did not drown. Many of the cattle survived. As a result, my parents witnessed to many.

We will have our own future trials. Will we each have the Word of God written in our hearts to keep us trusting and worshipping the Lord God?

Helen Dick Burton

Our Sure Foundation

As fire reveals the difference between gold, silver, and precious stones, and wood, hay, and stubble, so the day of judgment will test characters, showing the difference between characters formed after Christ's likeness and characters formed after the likeness of the selfish heart. All selfishness, all false religion, will then appear as it is. The worthless material will be consumed; but the gold of true, simple, humble faith will never lose its value. It can never be consumed; for it is imperishable.[33]

Character is not obtained by receiving an education. Character is not obtained by amassing wealth or by gaining worldly honor. Character is not obtained by having others fight the battle of life for us. It must be sought, worked for, fought for; and it requires a purpose, a will, a determination. To form a character which God will approve requires persevering effort. It will take a continual resisting of the powers of darkness to . . . have our names retained in the book of life. Is it not worth more to have our names registered in that book, have them immortalized among the heavenly angels, than to have them sounded in praise throughout the whole earth?[34]

In the probationary time granted us here we are each building a structure that is to have the inspection of the Judge of all the earth. This work is the molding of our characters. Every act of our lives is a stone in that building, every faculty is a worker, every blow that is struck is for good or for evil. The words of inspiration warn us to take heed how we build, to see that our foundation is sure. If we build upon the solid rock, pure, noble, upright deeds, the structure will go up beautiful and symmetrical, a fit temple for the indwelling of the Holy Spirit.[35]

Ellen G. White

For other foundation can no man lay than that is laid, which is Jesus Christ. Now if any man build upon this foundation gold, silver, precious stones, wood, hay, stubble; every man's work shall be made manifest: for the day shall declare it, because it shall be revealed by fire; and the fire shall try every man's work of what sort it is.

1 Corinthians 3:11-13.

God's Strength Is Made Perfect in Our Weakness

It had been a grueling contest, and I and my clients, who had put so much trust in me, had lost an important round. I sat in my car outside the courthouse and offered a silent prayer for the Holy Spirit's guidance as I randomly opened my Bible. My eye fell on the words "And he said unto me, My grace is sufficient for thee: for my strength is made perfect in weakness."

Then Your strength must be great, I thought, *for I have never felt so weak!* Just the day before I had received notice that my motion for summary judgment had been denied. Now dread filled me as thoughts of the gloating opposing counsel flooded my mind. He will be even more obnoxious than usual. What am I going to do now? This will result in a protracted trial that will be a hardship for my clients, both financially and emotionally. This I had hoped to avoid.

Reluctantly I slowly made my way to the courtroom, where the case was set for a status conference. Neither party nor other counsel had arrived. Taking a seat on a bench, I closed my eyes and prayed, "I trust You, Lord. I don't know how You are going to do it, but I trust You."

Opposing counsel and our clients arrived. A clerk directed us to come confer with the judge. *Here it comes,* I thought. *Counsel is going to slam me for losing, and the judge is going to try to push for a settlement less advantageous than my clients deserve.* How I dreaded this.

The judge greeted us and began. "I have reviewed this matter, and you two should be able to work out a settlement that will satisfy everyone. A little give-and-take is all you need." Not one word about the denied summary judgment motion. Not a word!

The judge left the room, and opposing counsel spoke. "I'm tired of this case. I could use the money a trial would generate, but my client isn't reasonable. I want to get this case over with as soon as possible." He then proposed a moderate settlement figure.

I silently thanked God, and the negotiation continued. The proposal was accepted by our clients, and an agreement for judgment was reached and executed. It was over!

God's strength was made perfect in my weakness! He had it all worked out before I even arrived at court. And He loved doing it! Just as earthly parents love it when their children turn to them and trust their counsel, so God loves it when we trust Him to keep His promises.

Jayne Strickland Colby

And he said unto me, My grace is sufficient for thee: for my strength is made perfect in weakness.

2 Corinthians 12:9.

Safe Harbor for Us and Our Children

Encourage one another, especially now that the day of his return is drawing near.

Hebrews 10:25, NLT.

Where is your handsome son?" asked the kindhearted gentleman. "Sonny is very spiritually sensitive, so I don't bring him to memorial services," I whispered. In his own way, Sonny had previously said his goodbye.

The church family had been sad because we knew that Doug, our brother and friend, was slipping away from cancer at age 53. Sonny hugged Pastor Lew before the congregation knelt together for the Garden of Prayer time. During the prayer Sonny, age 23, shed some tears. He was following his heart without knowing why or who needed our prayers. Because of his significant developmental disabilities the concept of death means absolutely nothing to Sonny.

The following day I went to the hospital chapel to pray with Doug's family. It was Glena, Doug's lovely wife, who uplifted my spirits. She told Doug's mother and sister about Sonny's developmental disabilities, and how he greets her with "Hi, Church" every time he sees her—regardless of where they are.

Laverne, Doug's sister, and I instantly became friends and comrades when I found out that she too has an autistic son. A few days later at his uncle's memorial service, I was blessed to meet handsome 13-year-old Rusten. Every day Christians with challenged children live life "on the front lines" in a war zone, and often we are wounded and in need of healing.

At Doug's service Pastor Lew shared these thoughts: People seem to enjoy sending off ships with fanfare and excitement, but seldom is there a crowd to greet the same ships when they return home. Doug and Glena had made a living as commercial fishermen, and Doug had proudly served in the 4th Canadian Ranger Patrol (similar to the U.S. Coast Guard).

Doug also served his church family with genuine affection. One of his jobs was church greeter, and he made us feel special. God's children are vessels; every day we go out into the sea of life not knowing what will happen to us. We are so blessed to be able to come to the church harbor where we should be able to safely love one another in the spirit of friendship until Jesus comes for us all.

Glena Knopp and Deborah Sanders

The Voice of Duty

The voice of duty is the voice of God—an inborn, heaven-sent guide. Whether it be pleasing or unpleasing, we are to do the duty that lies directly in our pathway. If the Lord would have us bear a message to Nineveh, it will not be pleasing to Him for us to go to Joppa or Capernaum. God has reasons for sending us to the place to which our feet are directed. . . .

It is the little foxes that spoil the vines; the little neglects, the little deficiencies, the little dishonesties, the little departures from principle, that blind the soul and separate it from God.

It is the little things of life that develop the spirit and determine the character. Those who neglect the little things will not be prepared to endure severe tests when they are brought to bear upon them. Remember that the character building is not finished till life ends. Every day a good or bad brick is placed in the structure. You are either building crookedly or with the exactness and correctness that will make a beautiful temple for God. Therefore, in looking for great things to do, neglect not the little opportunities that come to you day by day. He who neglects the little things, and yet flatters himself that he is ready to do wonderful things for the Master, is in danger of failing altogether. Life is made up, not of great sacrifices and of wonderful achievements, but of little things.[36]

Whatever your hands find to do, do it with your might. Make your work pleasant with songs of praise. If you would have a clean record in the books of heaven, never fret or scold. Let your daily prayer be, "Lord, help me to do my best. . . . Give me energy and cheerfulness. Help me to bring into my service the loving ministry of the Savior."

Look upon every duty, however humble, as sacred because it is part of God's service. Do not allow anything to make you forgetful of God. Bring Christ into all that you do. Then your lives will be filled with brightness and thanksgiving. You will do your best, moving forward cheerfully in the service of the Lord, your hearts filled with His joy.[37]

Ellen G. White

Whatsoever thy hand findeth to do, do it with thy might.

Ecclesiastes 9:10.

Navigating the Chaos

Upon leaving the marketplace in Nairobi, Kenya, my friend and I were besieged on every side by beggars of all ages and needs. As we navigated our way through this maze, we were thankful that our missionary friends had arranged for a local person to escort us.

Suddenly I saw an unusual sight; a tall, well-built man carrying a smaller, apparently crippled man on his back. The smaller man's legs were wrapped around the tall man's waist. They wove in and out of traffic with such agility that there was no time to assess their situation. I lost sight of them, but several times that day I wondered about them. Safely back at the school in Nairobi, we breathed a sigh of relief for surviving the trip through such traffic. That night at the fireplace as we recounted our experiences of the day, my friends Lydia and Newton asked, "By the way, did you see a tall, well-built man carrying a crippled man on his back?"

"As a matter of fact, I did!"

My friends informed me, "The 'hitchhiker' can see—he navigates the tall blind man through traffic, directing him to likely places to receive alms."

For a while I could not respond, pondering the ingenuity of these two persons with disabilities who had figured out a way to pool their resources, talents, and blessings for the benefit of them both. The blind man could not have lasted five minutes in the Nairobi traffic swirling out from the airport. Neither would have the crippled man been able to move more than a few feet on his own, soon dying of starvation, given the competition.

The Bible says "two are better than one, because they have a good reward for their labor" (Ecclesiasties 4:9, NKJV). In the body of Christ we are all members, although we are not given the same gifts and talents. Let us use the talents God has given us for the edifying of the whole body.

Vashti Hinds-Vanie

For just as each of us has one body with many members, and these members do not all have the same function, so in Christ we, though many, form one body, and each member belongs to all the others. We have different gifts, according to the grace given to each of us.

Romans 12:4-6, NIV.

Can God Really Use *Me*?

It was 7:00 one Thursday evening when I finally returned to the office to tidy my desk and collect my things before going home. After I had been in the office for about 10 minutes, the secretary and her little daughter came in. She arranged a few things on her desk, then wished me a good night as they left for home.

After spending a few more minutes in the office, I locked the door and walked toward my car. As I went, I thought about the two of them. The sun had already set and it was dark, and although I lived in the opposite direction I decided that if I saw them as I drove toward the gate of the campus I would offer to take them home.

No sooner had I driven off than I saw them walking toward the gate. After inviting them into the car, I took them to their home. When I stopped at their gate, the secretary said, "I must tell you something."

"What is it?" I asked.

She explained, "When I left the office, I had gone to the restroom to pray. I asked God to send us a ride home. You see, this morning I had forgotten to take the money for our taxi fare. If you had not given us a ride, we would have had to walk home in the dark."

I could hardly believe my ears. I said, "You mean that God used me to answer your prayer for a ride home?" She assured me that He did.

Right there I thanked God for using me that evening to answer the prayer of His child.

This incident has led me to think of the many times that perhaps God put a thought in my mind so that I could offer assistance to one of His children and I have dismissed it. My reason might have been that I would be inconvenienced, or it was not important, or it was not my business anyway.

As I think about the experience I humbly pray, "Dear Lord, give me ears to hear the cry of Your children, a heart that is sensitive to the needs of those around me, and the willingness to always perform the tasks that You want me to do."

Carol Joy Fider

True Beauty

There is a natural tendency with all to be sentimental rather than practical. In view of this fact, it is important that parents, in the education of their children, should direct and train their minds to love truth, duty, and self-denial, and to possess noble independence, to choose to be right, if the majority choose to be wrong. . . .

If they preserve to themselves sound constitutions and amiable tempers, they will possess true beauty that they can wear with a divine grace. And they will have no need to be adorned with artificials, for these are always expressive of an absence of the inward adorning of true moral worth. A beautiful character is of value in the sight of God. Such beauty will attract, but not mislead. Such charms are fast colors; they never fade.

The pure religion of Jesus requires of its followers the simplicity of natural beauty and the polish of natural refinement and elevated purity, rather than the artificial and false.[38]

There is an ornament that will never perish, that will promote the happiness of all around us in this life, and will shine with undimmed luster in the immortal future. It is the adorning of a meek and lowly spirit. . . . Of how little value are gold or pearls or costly array in comparison with the loveliness of Christ. Natural loveliness consists in symmetry, or the harmonious proportion of parts, each with the other; but spiritual loveliness consists in the harmony or likeness of our souls to Jesus. This will make its possessor more precious than fine gold, even the golden wedge of Ophir. The grace of Christ is indeed a priceless adornment. It elevates and ennobles its possessor and reflects beams of glory upon others, attracting them also to the Source of light and blessing.[39]

Ellen G. White

And let the beauty of the Lord our God be upon us.

Psalm 90:17.

Blessed by Family

My birthday was coming up in August. At age 50 I was reaching a real milestone. My plans weren't big—simply to get outdoors to hike and enjoy nature. Usually my husband, Cal, takes the day of my birthday off from work, and we spend it together doing outdoor activities. I was looking forward to doing the same this year. It's nice to feel pampered once in a while, and especially on birthdays. Receiving the many cards and calls from family and friends creates a warm feeling inside of being loved and cared for.

Well, this birthday turned out even more special than I ever dreamed. Lately Cal had been doing extra things around the house. He had cleaned the carpet on the outside porch—a big job that took him way past midnight to complete. I also saw him doing a lot of yard work, but I just thought, *He's doing this just because it needs to be done.* Even our youngest son, Dmitri, vacuumed the living room, and when I asked him why, he said, "Dad told me to do it." Again I thought, *How nice—getting help with the many chores around here.*

Late Sunday afternoon Cal called to me, saying, "Someone is coming up the drive." I turned around and saw a big SUV roll into our yard. My family had made the 13-hour trip from New York for my birthday! I watched them get out of the vehicle—my mom, my sister, and my brother-in-law—but I couldn't believe my eyes. They were actually standing in front of me! I had no clue they were coming. Never in my wildest dreams had I thought they would. All I could think of was that they had come for me. They had come to be with me. An overwhelming feeling of joy filled me inside. We spent time together, connecting in a closer way. What my family did for me is etched in my mind and heart. Just thinking about it makes me cry.

Yes, my birthday arrived with many gifts and surprises, but the most precious was that we were together. One day Jesus is going to surprise us, isn't He? One day He's coming from heaven to this earth just for you and just for me, and that is a day we will never forget. We will be together with our forever family for eternity. What a time that will be when He comes again! Just thinking about it makes me cry.

Rosemarie Clardy

How precious also
are thy thoughts unto
me, O God!
how great is the
sum of them!
Psalm 139:17.

The Gift of Gap-filling

I looked for someone among them who would build up the wall and stand before me in the gap.

Ezekiel 22:30, NIV.

I had just started working as a volunteer family therapist at Charis, a Christian counseling center in a tiny, economically deprived town in Fife, Scotland. The prayer team had invited me to an evening on which they would pray for me and ask God to bless my ministry. The day of the prayer meeting I'd been busy, and we were running late. I was tired, stressed, and frustrated. As we drove along I was complaining because I felt that all I ever did was fill gaps. Whenever I volunteered to help I would say, "I'll just fill in the gaps until you know what everyone else wants to do." And I was usually happy to do that. But somehow my identity felt lost in the "gap-filler" label, as if I was some kind of home-maintenance product.

The prayer team had been praying specifically for me before the meeting. They came with passages of Scripture, messages, encouragement, blessings, and insights. But one woman was a little hesitant. "I know this sounds kind of funny," she said, "but I feel God is calling you to be a gap-filler." *M'mm, that's interesting—I've just been complaining about being one of those.* She continued. "Maybe it's because without someone filling the gaps, things fall apart." I looked at the old walls of the building where irregular Scottish rocks had been carefully piled together. There was no way they could be fitted snugly to keep out the winds and wild weather, so mortar had been carefully inserted between the stones to keep the building safe, strong, and warm. I looked at a small, wooden cross that stood on a table. Yes, Jesus had also been an amazing gap-filler: He filled the gap between earth and heaven, death and life.

Most of my gap-filling activities are not courageous, dramatic, or lifesaving. A cake for a funeral. A freshly laundered tablecloth. A bag of toothbrushes for a local homeless project. The scripture reading. A dish for the potluck. Maybe a few words of friendship and encouragement. A simple prayer. But although gap-filling is invisible, it's also essential and it needs people who are flexible enough to fill the different-shaped gaps—like the mortar in the stone wall.

I wonder if there's a spiritual gift of gap-filling designed for those of us who do this work. And maybe Jesus would say, "Blessed are the gap-fillers, for they prevent things from falling apart." What gap is God calling you to fill today?

Karen Holford

The Royal Robe

The parable of the wedding garment [Matthew 22:1-14] opens before us a lesson of the highest consequence. . . . By the wedding garment in the parable is represented the pure, spotless character which Christ's true followers will possess. . . . The fine linen, says the Scripture, "is the righteousness of saints." It is the righteousness of Christ, His own unblemished character, that through faith is imparted to all who receive Him as their personal Savior.

The white robe of innocence was worn by our first parents when they were placed by God in holy Eden. They lived in perfect conformity to the will of God. . . . A beautiful soft light, the light of God, enshrouded the holy pair. . . . But when sin entered, they severed their connection with God, and the light that had encircled them departed. Naked and ashamed, they tried to supply the place of the heavenly garments by sewing together fig leaves for a covering.[40]

We cannot provide a robe of righteousnesses for ourselves, for the prophet says, "All our righteousnesses are as filthy rags" (Isaiah 64:6). There is nothing in us from which we can clothe the soul so that its nakedness shall not appear. We are to receive the robe of righteousness woven in the loom of heaven, even the spotless robe of Christ's righteousness.[41]

God has made ample provision that we may stand perfect in His grace, wanting in nothing, waiting for the appearing of our Lord. Are you ready? Have you the wedding garment on? That garment will never cover deceit, impurity, corruption, or hypocrisy. The eye of God is upon you. It is a discerner of the thoughts and intents of the heart. We may conceal our sins from the eyes of men, but we can hide nothing from our Maker.[42]

Let the youth and the little children be taught to choose for themselves that royal robe woven in heaven's loom—the "fine linen, clean and white," which all the holy ones of earth will wear. This robe, Christ's own spotless character, is freely offered to every human being. But all who receive it will receive and wear it here.[43]

Ellen G. White

And to her was granted that she should be arrayed in fine linen, clean and white: for the fine linen is the righteousness of saints.

Revelation 19:8.

You Received the Bigger Blessing?

I am picky about my "coffee" mugs. They have to be the right shape, the right weight, the design has to be appealing, and the inside has to be a light color. I had a drawer full of mugs at work—some I loved, some I didn't, plus one for every mood and season!

It was just after Christmas, and I was sitting in the staff room one afternoon sipping tea out of a relatively new mug that was quickly becoming my favorite. One of my colleagues admired the cup and asked where I had bought it. She then went on to say that she had received pajamas and a robe for Christmas with the identical color and design. We laughed, and I assured her that my mug had not been bought as part of a pajama set.

When I went back to my office a thought started to repeat itself in my mind, *Jill, go and give Esther your mug.*

What? Give away my beautiful mug? *Yes, Jill, give your mug to Esther.* But, but, but . . . I came up with all sorts of excuses to keep my beloved mug.

I quickly realized how selfish I was being over a silly mug. Without any more thought I marched down to Esther's office and gave her my mug. I told her how much fun it would be for her to sip coffee out of a mug that matched her pajamas and robe. She didn't really want to take it, but I insisted.

The next morning, Esther appeared in my office with a little card and a book of poetry as a way of thanking me.

After saying, "Have a great day," Esther left my office, but right away she turned around and came back. Standing in my doorway, she said, "I haven't told anyone this except my husband, but I am scheduled for a lung biopsy in two weeks. The gift of your mug yesterday meant so much to me. It represented more than a mug. It told me that people care about me. It means so much to me, and I don't know how I can ever thank you."

As we hugged and talked for a few more minutes, I was overjoyed that I had listened to God and His prompting to give away my mug. I'm not sure who received the bigger blessing!

Jill Rhynard

A generous person will prosper; whoever refreshes others will be refreshed.

Proverbs 11:25, NIV.

Letting Christ Shine Through

I can do all this through him who gives me strength.

Philippians 4:13, NIV.

My sister died last week. When at my sister's house, I noticed her walker-on-wheels by the garage door. I took a picture of it to remind me that in heaven she will literally run and not get weary. Yes, Lynne without hospice, IVs, prosthesis, surgeons, neurologists, prescriptions, canes, and pain. As I said the day she died, "I'll have a sister again on resurrection morning. She'll be better than new!" And as I said to her at her casket, "I'll see you in the morning."

Lynne's death gives new life to the Scriptures for me. The night before she died she requested to hear the hymn "Blessed Assurance." And now she indeed rests assured. Lynne resides in a gravesite on a hilltop that overlooks a river. It's her well-deserved rest. There was no cure for her cancer and neuromuscular disease, but I remember reading that rest was the only remedy that could alleviate her symptoms. She is now resting. But not for long!

The week before Lynne died I received a story of grief and gratitude. It was a testament to Lynne, who was a quilter herself. It seems that a woman faced her Maker at the last judgment. Before her, and other women, their lives lay like the squares of a quilt. An angel sat sewing the quilt squares into a tapestry of the life. The woman reported, "But as my angel took each piece of cloth, I noticed how ragged and torn my squares were. Each was labeled with a part of my life that had been difficult—the challenges and illnesses that I'd faced, the hardships making the biggest holes of all. I glanced around. Nobody else had such squares. Other than a tiny hole here and there, the other tapestries were filled with bright hues of color. My heart sank.

"Finally, it was time for each life to be displayed, held up to the light. Each woman held up her tapestry. Their lives seemed so filled. Then my angel nodded for me to rise.

"When I stood and lifted to the light the combined squares of my life, everyone gasped. As I looked upon my life's tapestry I saw that light flooded through the many holes, creating an image. It was the face of Christ. 'Every time you gave your life over to Me, it became My life, My hardship, My struggle,' Jesus said. 'Each point of light in your life is when you stepped aside and let Me shine through.'"

So loved ones, may all your quilts be threadbare and worn, so Christ can shine through!

Diane Shellyn Nudd

It Takes Time

The mind of a man or a woman does not come down in a moment from purity and holiness to depravity, corruption, and crime. It takes time to transform the human to the divine, or to degrade those formed in the image of God to the brutal or the satanic. By beholding we become changed. Though formed in the image of his Maker, man can so educate his mind that sin which he once loathed will become pleasant to him. As he ceases to watch and pray, he ceases to guard the citadel, the heart. . . . Constant war against the carnal mind must be maintained; and we must be aided by the refining influence of the grace of God, which will attract the mind upward and habituate it to meditate upon pure and holy things.[44]

Character does not come by chance. It is not determined by one outburst of temper, one step in the wrong direction. It is the repetition of the act that causes it to become habit, and molds the character either for good or for evil. Right characters can be formed only by persevering, untiring effort, by improving every entrusted talent and capability to the glory of God.[45]

God expects us to build characters in accordance with the pattern set before us. We are to lay brick by brick, adding grace to grace, finding our weak points and correcting them in accordance with the directions given.[46]

God gives us strength, reasoning power, time, in order that we may build characters on which He can place His stamp of approval. He desires each child of His to build a noble character, by the doing of pure, noble deeds, that in the end he may present a symmetrical structure, a fair temple, honored by man and God. . . .

He who would grow into a beautiful building for the Lord must cultivate every power of the being. It is only by the right use of the talents that the character can be developed harmoniously. Thus we bring to the foundation that which is represented in the Word as gold, silver, precious stones—material that will stand the test of God's purifying fires.[47]

Ellen G. White

I the Lord do keep it; I will water it every moment: lest any hurt it, I will keep it night and day.

Isaiah 27:3.

Mother's Answered Prayer

The winter months in Woodland Park, Michigan, can be very cold. Sometimes the temperature drops to 20 degrees below zero, and the snow is often more than three feet deep. My nine siblings and I were raised in Woodland Park, and because our father worked in another state to support the family, our mother raised us mostly alone.

The following is a true account of an incident that happened when we were children. It happened on one of those cold days when the snow was too deep for anyone to come to our house to bring the wood we burned to heat our house.

"I had put the last pieces of wood in the stove," Mother recalled, "and I prayed, 'Lord, this is the last of the wood. When it's gone, my children and I could freeze. Please help us. In Jesus' name.'"

"Then," Mother said, "I sat in a chair, looking out the window, meditating. Seemingly out of nowhere, a wagon, drawn by two red horses, came up to the house. A young man wearing a red cap was riding on the wagon that was loaded with wood. It seemed as if the horses pulled the wagon over the snow with no effort at all. The young man unloaded the wood, returned to the wagon, and left without a word. I never saw him again. The wood lasted until the weather broke."

God answers prayers in many ways and in His own time. Sometimes He answers immediately and miraculously in dire situations, such as was experienced by our mother.

Every time I think about this incident my faith is renewed, knowing God's promises are true and faithful. He can, and will, do anything if it is His will.

I thank God for a mother who believed in prayer and who taught us to pray. Until she passed away at the age of 91, she was a faithful prayer warrior and loved studying the Bible.

We can know that God is always there for us, especially in times of need. Just trust His Word, which promises, "The Lord is good, a refuge in times of trouble. He cares for those who trust in him" (Nahum 1:7, NIV).

Moselle Slaten Blackwell

> If ye shall ask any thing in my name, I will do it.
>
> John 14:14.

Apples of Gold

Four o'clock in the morning wasn't usually the busiest hour for this coastal restaurant. But that changed when my marine biology class, out on a field trip, filed through their doors. The only server there, a girl probably in her late teens, looked at us wide-eyed as one by one chairs and tables began filling up with college students. I secretly wondered how she would handle this unexpected influx of business.

I watched with interest as she went to each table, taking orders and answering questions. Then she came to my table. She displayed a pleasant demeanor while doing an excellent job of handling such a group, and I told her so.

She looked at me and with hope in her voice, exclaimed, "Oh, would you please tell that to my boss? I've been trying to get on the day shift, and that would really help." I assured her I'd be happy to do that.

When I went to pay my bill, I mentioned to the cashier the fine work the server did in serving so many people. She yanked a paper towel from the nearby dispenser, grabbed a pencil, and slapped both on the counter in front of me. "Please," she begged, her hands shaking with excitement, "would you write that down for our boss to see? I'd appreciate it so much!" That lowly paper towel almost took on a life of its own as I recorded every complimentary thing I noticed about this young server.

Jesus tells us about the importance of appreciation in the Bible story about 10 lepers. These men came to Jesus asking for mercy. When He saw them, Jesus told them to go and show themselves to the priests. On the way they were cleansed, but only one leper came back to thank Him. The Lord showed disappointment that the other nine didn't do the same. The leper who returned to offer thanks glorified God by acknowledging that the gift of healing came from Him.

In this fast-paced world, where technology often bypasses face-to-face communication, it's easy to take for granted the little things that people do to help us. One kind word or act, no matter how small, may be just what is needed to change a person's outlook, circumstance, or life.

God gives us many blessings daily. We glorify God when we thank Him for the privilege of sharing these blessings.

Marcia Mollenkopf

What a Reward!

Glorious will be the reward bestowed when the faithful workers gather about the throne of God and of the Lamb. When John in his mortal state beheld the glory of God, he fell as one dead; he was not able to endure the sight. But when the children of God shall have put on immortality, they will "see him as he is" (1 John 3:2). They will stand before the throne, accepted in the Beloved. All their sins have been blotted out, all their transgressions borne away. Now they can look upon the undimmed glory of the throne of God. They have been partakers with Christ in His sufferings, they have been workers together with Him in the plan of redemption, and they are partakers with Him in the joy of seeing souls saved in the kingdom of God, there to praise God through all eternity. . . .

In that day the redeemed will shine forth in the glory of the Father and the Son. The angels, touching their golden harps, will welcome the King and His trophies of victory. . . . A song of triumph will peal forth, filling all heaven. Christ has conquered. He enters the heavenly courts, accompanied by His redeemed ones, the witnesses that His mission of suffering and sacrifice has not been in vain. . . .

There are homes for the pilgrims of earth. There are robes for the righteous, with crowns of glory and palms of victory. All that has perplexed us in the providences of God will in the world to come be made plain. The things hard to be understood will then find explanation. The mysteries of grace will unfold before us. Where our finite minds discovered only confusion and broken promises, we shall see the most perfect and beautiful harmony. We shall know that infinite love ordered the experiences that seemed most trying. As we realize the tender care of Him who makes all things work together for our good, we shall rejoice with joy unspeakable and full of glory.[48]

I urge you to prepare for the coming of Christ in the clouds of heaven. . . . Prepare for the judgment, that when Christ shall come, to be admired in all them that believe, you may be among those who will meet Him in peace.[49]

Ellen G. White

> If any man's work abide . . . , he shall receive a reward.
>
> 1 Corinthians 3:14.

A Face to Remember

My trip to Italy was a memorable experience. However, the first five days were a little more memorable than I would have wished for. I was scheduled for the 12-day trip to conduct workshops. I left Washington, D.C., at 3:00 p.m. on a Wednesday afternoon, and arrived at my final destination in Italy (after four different flights) Thursday afternoon. Unfortunately, I got only a couple hours' sleep on the plane. I collapsed in my bed at 7:00 p.m., eagerly anticipating a solid night's sleep. I awoke at 10:30 p.m., wide-eyed and far from falling back to sleep.

This pattern occurred for five nights. The stress on my body from lack of sleep, lack of exercise, a change in eating habits, and conducting back-to-back workshops while having to be translated took their toll. By Sunday evening the cortisol levels in my body were so high that I experienced an eczematic reaction. Half my face was red, swollen, and itchy. In addition to the physiological effects of the flare-up were the psychological effects: I looked about 10 years older—and my ego was not handling this well. I don't feel the need to look 20 years old when I'm in my mid-40s, but I also don't like the idea of looking like I'm in my mid-50s, either!

After another flight and suffering the loss of my luggage, I settled in at Villa Aurora, the college in Florence, where I was to teach a couple of classes for the seminary students for several days. It was here that I began to heal. But healing isn't always confined to the physical.

At breakfast one morning I sat with Laura, one of the seminary students. I knew very little Italian, and she very little English. But through helping each other we were able to communicate well. At one point in our conversation she looked at me, used her hand to make a circle in front of her face, and said, "You have a peaceful face."

At that moment I came to see my vanity for what it was. I had been feeling anxious because my face looked older than it should. But now I realized that in spite of all that stress and anxiety—possibly even because of it—God could work to allow others to see what really mattered: the fruit of His Spirit. This experience made me realize that when all is said and done, the memorable moments for those with whom we come in contact will be the times we have allowed God to work through us so others can see His face. His face is much more memorable than mine.

Bonita Joyner Shields

> For now we see in a mirror, dimly, but then we will see face to face.
>
> 1 Corinthians 13:12, NRSV.

Take Me Home

But our citizenship is in heaven. And we eagerly await a Savior from there, the Lord Jesus Christ.

Philippians 3:20, NIV.

I was homeless by the age of 3 when my family became refugees because Communists had taken over my homeland of Estonia. The KGB targeted my father, who was the church president for that area and considered to be a leader of the people. Therefore our lives were imperiled. We fled, just the four of us in my family, leaving behind our homeland, extended family and friends, my father's work for the church, and all that was familiar and treasured. Consequently, my earliest memories involve a loss and recovery. I lost the treasure of having relatives and felt like a blown-away leaf from a family tree. I knew firsthand the reality of threat to life and experienced terrors represented by sounds and images—bombings, sirens, flight, fire, screams, the destruction of what humankind had built and the destruction of what God had made. My losses were represented by enormity—country, family, identity—as well as by minutiae: basic essentials of life, the few toys I possessed, the few friends I could make in our wanderings.

Then we arrived in what, for us, was the "promised land." We found refuge in America, and our wanderings were over. Eventually, however, the unexpected happened. The Soviet Union fell apart, and I could return to my homeland. I could rediscover my identity, my people, my relatives, my language, my beautiful country. This unplanned gift, so to speak, brought a richness to my life I had never expected.

More important, I learned more fully the lessons of loss and recovery, of roots and returns, and I could apply these more readily to our experience as Christians who are looking toward our return to a homeland that God has promised us. By sin we were cut off from our originally intended roots. But God isn't happy with the "refugee" experiences we must endure and therefore has a better place for us; things we haven't dreamed of are waiting for us.

Just as it was my choice to return to my roots, we can look ahead to a return to our heavenly homeland. I am grateful for my United States citizenship, so significant when my own country was destroyed, but my life was enriched and became whole when I could reclaim the citizenship of my roots. In the same way we can look forward to our citizenship in heaven, which we will receive when our Lord returns and takes us home.

Lilya Wagner

How We Are to Work

In daily doing the works of Christ, it becomes a pleasure to do His will. Christ came to our world to live out the law of God, to be our pattern in all things. He placed Himself between the mercy seat, and the vast number of heartless worshippers who were full of ostentation, pride, and vanity, and by His lessons of truth, which were "eloquent with simplicity," He impressed the people with the necessity of spiritual worship. His lessons were impressive, beautiful and weighty with importance, and yet so simple that a child could understand them. The truth He presented was so deep that the wisest and most accomplished teacher could never exhaust it. Those who work as seeing the Invisible will always preserve simplicity, charging the simplest words with the power of the grandest truths.[50]

The youth may be a power for Christ, if they will maintain their simplicity, and not seek to present something startling, something original, but teach the precepts of their Lord. But to invest the simplest truths with novelty and singularity is to rob them of their power to win souls to Christ. . . . The use of long words and soaring eloquence is not essential to success. What you need is a living experience in the things of God, and simplicity in presenting the love of Christ to the lost. . . . When the heart is aglow with the love of Jesus, you will express it to others, and become witnesses for Christ.[51]

We are not to hide the gospel, or cover the cross of Christ with ornamental roses and thus make the preaching of it of no effect.[52]

The true, honest expression of a son or daughter of God, spoken in natural simplicity, has power to unbolt the door to hearts that have long been closed against Christ and His love.[53]

Ellen G. White

But sanctify the Lord God in your hearts: and be ready always to give an answer to every man that asketh you a reason of the hope that is in you with meekness and fear.

1 Peter 3:15.

Living in the Moment

I've decided that whatever I do, I want it to be useful. I'm a grandmother and do not have much time to waste. If there's something in life that I have failed to do or learn, now is the moment to do it or learn it. Therefore, while I take care of my little granddaughter Julie, I also want to do something useful.

While I watch her, I read a book, but I barely read two paragraphs before my attention is distracted. She's learning to stand up, and recently she learned to sit up by herself. She also turns and swivels fearlessly. I try to embroider some Christmas presents, but after a few stitches I have to stop and help her. I cannot leave her alone with her toys. A month ago she would play quietly with her hands and her stuffed toys. Now she can crawl anywhere in the house. And so I can read, I can embroider, or I can watch Julie.

I'm afraid that she will hurt herself. She totally disregards danger. She throws herself from her stroller to retrieve whatever fell out. I use the seat belt, but she slides around, and suddenly I notice she's dangling half out, kicking and laughing. How much will I get done this morning? I finally realize it—nothing, nothing except to be with Julie.

So what is it that I can learn from this? There is no experience in our lives that is meaningless in the eyes of God. Today I can give love, caresses, and hugs. *Thank You, Lord. There are many who do not have that.* There's nothing like the joy of rocking Julie so that she sleeps trustingly in my arms; nothing like the pleasure of guiding her first steps and reliving the beautiful moments with my own children as I care for my grandchild.

Patience is an important lesson I must continue learning, and lessons of quietness of spirit. Today I will remain calm, without turmoil. I will find quietness for my soul, and I will know God. I also have learned God's love and care toward me as I care for Julie. This is the greatest privilege and the best lesson—to understand what God does for me and for each of us every day. I have learned much through this experience.

Consider your challenges today, no matter what they are. What lesson do you think God is trying to teach you?

Leni Uría de Zamorano

> Be still and know that I am God.
>
> Psalm 46:10, NKJV.

Give It to God

I love the Lord,

because he hath

heard my voice and

my supplications.

Because he hath

inclined his ear

unto me, therefore

will I call upon him as

long as I live.

Psalm 116:1, 2.

It was late one Saturday night, and I had returned home from spending the evening with some friends. My life was going quite well, yet I found myself feeling sad and even crying a bit about my loneliness. Life as a single woman was not what I had pictured for myself from the time I was a young girl. I had always dreamed of being married and having a family. As the kind of person who always wants to "fix" everything for everyone, I had spent several years trying to fix that loneliness piece in my life. Needless to say, my efforts failed, and I found myself reasonably happy, yet lonely.

As an educator I had had the opportunity to learn some psychology, and deep down I knew that one of my problems was that I always tried to make things work out. While that can be a good thing, it is not always within one's capabilities to "fix" everything.

Finally, that evening as I lay in bed crying, I prayed to God and asked Him to help me be content with being single. That was the first time I had ever uttered those words. I followed those words up with "or bring someone into my life." Usually, I asked Him to bring someone into my life to make me happy. Sleep followed, and I awoke the next day with a bit of a new view of life.

On Monday evening I received a call from a man who said that we had a mutual friend and that he would like to meet me and go out for dinner. I agreed.

Tuesday was met with a bit of anxiety and skepticism about going on a blind date at my age. I convinced myself that one date couldn't hurt and that, likely, I wouldn't be interested in him anyway.

The evening of our first date arrived, and I answered the door to see the kindest, gentlest, most loving man I had ever met. He stood there with a dozen roses for me—and the rest is history. We've been married for 17 years, and I tell everyone that "God smiled on me when He brought my husband into my life."

I thank God every day for bringing me and my husband together. I just needed to give all to Jesus.

Karen J. Johnson

The Lord Is My Shepherd

The whole of Psalm 23 gives me great comfort. I can meditate on it and find meaning in every situation in which I find myself. When I am overwhelmed by life's storms, I sometimes forget to pray, and all His promises make no sense. But when I finally call to my God in prayer, His hand does lead me beside the still waters. He leads me to peace, and my mind is at rest even if the storm still rages.

Part of verse 3 says, "He leads me in the paths of righteousness for His name's sake" (NKJV). Sometimes, when in distress or upset because of earthly problems, we can do wrong or sinful things, but if we constantly cling to Him and remember His promises, He will keep us from doing wrong. Verse 4 goes on to say, "Yea, though I walk through the valley of the shadow of death, I will fear no evil; . . . Your rod and Your staff, they comfort me" (NKJV). A while back I was admitted to the hospital, facing death in the eyes, but because my beloved biological family and my church family were praying for me I was at peace, even in the midst of pain. I knew my condition could be fatal, but I did not fear death, because God was comforting me.

According to verse 5, "You prepare a table before me in the presence of my enemies; You anoint my head with oil; my cup runs over" (NKJV). So many times God helps us achieve things that the people who look down on us think we never could achieve. But because He loves us, God will bring good things to us even as our enemies watch. We will rejoice all the while as our lives overflow with His blessings.

Verse 6 is so comforting: "Surely goodness and mercy shall follow me all the days of my life; and I will dwell in the house of the Lord forever" (NKJV). To me this means that every day, no matter where I might be, I am wrapped in His love and am divinely protected. Praise God, this also means I will be His forever.

Sisters, there are so many ups and downs in life, but wherever you are, whatever the situation, remember that God loves you and will work through you if you allow Him to do so. You will see Him working and turning your situation around.

Peggy Rusike

He makes me to lie down in green pastures; He leads me beside the still waters.

Psalm 23:2, NKJV.

So Many Blessings!

Some time ago during our morning devotion we read about a woman who in times of great distress had made a decision to begin a "Blessing Journal." This got me thinking about the many blessings in my life, wondering if there was a way I could record them so that they'd be there to remind me of God's goodness when I lapse into a state of ingratitude and complaining.

There is the blessing of my husband and son. There are times when things are difficult in the day-to-day existence and the realities of marriage stare me in the face, and my beautiful child gets on my last existing half a nerve. Then I remember how aimless my life was without them, and how they are a direct answer to many prayers I've prayed.

I thank God for my mother who is such a blessing to me and my family. At times she wants me to take her places with no regard to my agenda, and I am tempted to fuss. Then I'm reminded of those who have no mother to visit or even call on the telephone. I also remember how much help she is to us in raising our son and doing all the cooking in our home.

I thank God for the blessing of good health and the ability to work. More often than not I complain about how busy I am and how tired I feel; then I am reminded of those who would like to get up and move around and cannot. Or those who want employment and can find no work.

I thank God for using me in His work, even though I may be a reluctant subject and complain bitterly about how hard it is. I thank Him that I can be a blessing to someone else.

My in-laws are another great blessing in my life. I often hear folks around me complaining about their in-laws, but I can do nothing but sing their praises. My father-in-law likes to say, "I have run out of receptacles to collect all the blessings the Lord is sending to me. I need to find some more." That quotation always encourages me and halts my complaining spirit.

Let's daily reflect on the little things that show us how blessed we are: the ability to breathe and get out of bed, the ability to walk, talk, work and get tired; mercies as we go about our daily activities; a loving and caring family.

Raylene McKenzie Ross

He will bless them that fear the Lord, both small and great. The Lord shall increase you more and more, you and your children. Ye are blessed of the Lord which made heaven and earth.

Psalm 115:13-15.

Good and Evil

The fear of the Lord is the beginning of wisdom; all who follow his precepts have good understanding.

Psalm 111:10, NIV.

When that serpent, the devil, told Eve that she would "be like God, knowing good and evil" (Genesis 3:5, NIV), I'm certain she had no idea what that meant—but she soon found out. Imagine the first animal death, the first fight with Adam, the death of her favorite flower. And then one son, her precious firstborn, killed his brother, Abel. She lost two sons that day. But there must have been good things happening, too—sweet babies born, joyful family gatherings, fun animal antics, and gorgeous sunrises and sunsets. There was still a lot that was good.

It seems that good and evil are always mixed up. My mother died two days after our daughter's birthday. Does one mourn or celebrate? Good and evil; our world is all mixed up. There is enough good that most days we enjoy our lives; life on this earth is not all that bad. But then someone close to us—or even we ourselves—gets cancer, or is maimed in an accident, or a loved one betrays trust, and we don't want to live here on this old earth anymore. Hour after hour, day after day, our televisions portray horrifying famines, earthquakes, floods, fires, crimes, war, and death. We don't want to know any more of evil! We want heaven where there will be no more heartache, "no more death or mourning or crying or pain, for the old order of things has passed away" (Revelation 21:4, NIV). Evil and good will no longer be mixed up.

Today's text tells us that "the fear of the Lord is the beginning of wisdom; all who follow his precepts have good understanding." What does that mean? How do we get that wisdom? I believe it means to keep God's laws—that is, to know good. One of the things I have always appreciated about God's rules is that they always make sense; they are for our good and happiness. They aren't arbitrary rules someone just made up. When we follow them, we are healthier and happier; our families are stronger and our communities are safer.

The fact that Eve couldn't imagine evil gave her no excuse. Neither do we have an excuse; God's plan has always been for us to know good. But ever since that day in the garden, Eve's sisters have known a lot of evil. Oh, how I wish that each and every one of them knew Jesus and His plan for their lives. And that is my wish for you today, too.

Ardis Dick Stenbakken

Shine With Living Brightness

Christians are Christ's jewels, bought with an infinite price. They are to shine brightly for Him, shedding forth the light of His loveliness. And ever they are to remember that all the luster that Christian character possesses is received from the Sun of Righteousness.

The luster of Christ's jewels depends on the polishing that they receive. God does not compel us to be polished. We are left free to choose to be polished or to remain unpolished. But everyone who is pronounced worthy of a place in the Lord's temple must submit to the polishing process. He must consent to have the sharp edges cut away from his character, that it may be shapely and beautiful, fitted to represent the perfection of Christ's character. . . .

The divine Worker spends little time on worthless material. Only the precious jewels does He polish after the similitude of a palace. With hammer and chisel He cuts away the rough edges, preparing us for a place in God's temple. The process is severe and trying. It hurts human pride. Christ cuts deep into the experience that man in his self-sufficiency regarded as complete, and takes away self-uplifting from the character. He cuts away the surplus surface, and, putting the stone to the polishing wheel, presses it close, that all roughness may be worn off. Then holding the jewel up to the light, the Master sees in it a reflection of His own image, and it is pronounced worthy of a place in His temple.

Blessed be the experience, however severe, that gives new value to the stone, enabling it to shine with living brightness!

[The Lord] has workers whom He will call forth from poverty and obscurity. Engaged in the common duties of life, and clothed with coarse raiment, they are looked upon by men as of little value. But Christ sees in them infinite possibilities, and in His hands they will become precious jewels, to shine brightly in the kingdom of God. "They shall be mine, saith the Lord of hosts, in that day when I make up my jewels" (Malachi 3:17).

Christ's perfect knowledge of human character fits Him to deal with minds. God knows just how to treat each soul. He judges not as man judges. He knows the real value of the material upon which He is working in fitting men and women for positions of trust.[54]

Ellen G. White

And they shall be mine, saith the Lord of hosts, in that day when I make up my jewels; and I will spare them, as a man spareth his own son that serveth him.

Malachi 3:17.

Why in the World Are We Here?

Several years ago I stood atop a windy hill in eastern Montana. Behind me was a graveyard. My grandparents slept there. My twin sisters. My uncles, aunts, cousins. All of them once lived in the valley at my feet where the Musselshell River winds its way through green fields of alfalfa.

My grandfather had come to this place from Norway, a vigorous young man, striding across the Montana prairie to establish his homestead. There, in the rainbow bend of the river, he built the barn, the bunkhouse, the log cabin in which his 13 children were born. And over there his sheep and cattle and horses grazed.

Nothing is there now except long grass, bending in the wind.

And I wondered, Who will remember that he was here at all? that his long life was well-lived? that he was a good man, an honest man, a true neighbor? Are the tombstones behind me the end of it all? Why was he here? Why are *we* here? How are we to fill the time between Homeleaving and Homecoming?

In a long-ago Eden garden God crouched beside a clay form so like His own, the form that would be Adam, the capstone of His creation. In one last touch before breathing the breath of life into the perfectly shaped nostrils, the great God of the universe bent over and touched that noble heart, instilling within it a piece of His own divinity: the desire to serve others. God knew that therein lay immortality. Therein lay happiness. Therein lay the assurance that in serving others Adam and his children would be remembered forever.

I think God has fun making people, chuckling to Himself as He tucks in the gift of singing here, or the ability to say just the right word there; laughing as He forms feet that simply can't stay still when happy music is playing, or shaping a brain that can make sense of Einstein's theory of relativity. Some of us may feel that His phone must have rung just as He was ready to give us our talent and that He became distracted. Or maybe we look at another's gift that's so obvious and so wonderful and say, "Why can't I do that?" Here's His reply: "All the days ordained for me were written in your book before one of them came to be" (Psalm 139:16, NIV).

Does that sound like Someone who didn't know what He was doing when He made you?

Jeannette Busby Johnson

How precious to me are your thoughts, God! How vast is the sum of them!

Psalm 139:17, NIV.

No Joy

God is our refuge
and strength,
a very present
help in trouble.

Psalm 46:1.

My life has been in turmoil recently. We have been going through a bad spot at church, and it has taken its toll on me. I usually sing, but I cannot find the joy that gives me the desire to sing. I am teaching a Bible class, and although they say I've been doing a good job, my heart has not been in it.

I started a new job, and I have been fighting to find my way—with very little success. We had two unexpectedly large expenditures that pushed our finances into disaster, and I do not see a way out. My brother-in-law died, my sister-in-law's mom died, and my mother got sick and was hospitalized for two weeks.

At home the air-conditioner is leaking and blowing hot air. I have not been focused, and my youngest child, for the first time, isn't doing her best in school. My oldest child senses the upheaval and has been clingy lately—a sure sign of stress.

Yesterday my husband walked in the door and announced that his car had died in the driveway. I wanted to curl up and cry, but of course I couldn't. I got the children to bed, called my dad, and asked to use Mom's car so we could get the girls to school and us to work.

I'm emotionally and physically exhausted. I can't take anymore. I slept last night but awoke with a stomachache, another sure sign of stress. As usual, I studied my Bible lesson guide, read my Bible, and then read the women's devotional book. Today's story was called "A Childlike Faith." It was just what I needed to read. It reminded me to trust God and have a childlike faith that He will take care of it all.

I finished getting ready for work and got into my mom's car. I like quiet first thing in the morning, but this morning I felt compelled to turn on the radio. Guess what God did for me? He played two songs that I needed to hear. The first stated, "Lift up your face. Salvation is calling." The second stated, "He has conquered." All I could do was cry.

I have never doubted that God loves me, but today He told me just what I needed to hear. He reminded me that He is still in control and that no matter how bad the situation, He is present, willing, and more than able! I gave it all to Him today. And guess what? I found my joy.

Tamara Marquez de Smith

Rough Stones Polished for a Holy Temple

Through the grace of Christ you will make decided endeavors to overcome all cold, rough, harsh, uncourteous ways and manners. . . .
The mighty cleaver of truth has taken you out of the quarry of the world. You were rough stones with jagged edges, bruising and marring whoever you came in contact with; there is a work to be done to smooth off the rough edges. If you appreciated the value of the work that is to be done in the workshop of God, you would welcome the blows of the ax and the hammer. Your self-esteem will be hurt, your high opinion of yourself will be cut away by the ax and the hammer, and the roughness of your character will be smoothed off; and when self and carnal propensities are worked away, then the stone will assume proper proportions for the heavenly building, and then the polishing, refining, subduing, burnishing processes will begin, and you will be molded after the model of Christ's character. His own image is to be reflected in the polished character of His human agent, and the stone is to be fitted for the heavenly building. . . .

If we are not better men and women, if we are not more kindhearted, more pitiful, more courteous, more full of tenderness and love; if we do not manifest to others the love that led Jesus to the world on His mission of mercy, we are not witnesses to the world of the power of Jesus Christ. Jesus lived not to please Himself. . . . He came to elevate, to ennoble, to make happy all with whom He came in contact. . . . He never did a rude action, never spoke a discourteous word.[55]

It is the privilege of every youth to make of his character a beautiful structure. . . . Seek the Lord most earnestly, that you may become more and more refined, more spiritually cultured.[56]

Ellen G. White

In whom all the building fitly framed together groweth unto an holy temple in the Lord.

Ephesians 2:21.

Live Righteously and Godly

O that our hearts may be deeply impressed with the importance of living holy lives, that the world may take knowledge of us that we have been with Jesus, and have learned of Him. Christian worth does not depend upon brilliant talents, lofty birth, wonderful powers, but on a clean heart—a heart which, purified and refined, reflects the image of divinity. It is the presence of Him who gave His life for us that makes the soul beautiful. . . . It is the men of prayer that are men of power. . . .

Do not allow trifling things to absorb your time and attention. Keep your mind on the glorious themes of the Word of God. A study of these themes will give you a strength that will carry you through the trials and difficulties of the last days, and bring you to where you will walk with Christ in white, because you are worthy. In the Word of God, studied and obeyed, we possess a spiritual guide and instructor by which the worst forms of evil in ourselves may be brought under the discipline of His law. If the teachings of this Word were made the controlling influence in our lives, if mind and heart were brought under its restraining power, the evils that now exist in churches and in families would find no place. Upon converted households the purest blessings would descend, and from these households an influence would go forth that would make God's people a power on the side of truth. . . .

Now is the time to watch and pray, to put away all self-indulgence, all pride, all selfishness. The precious moments that are now by many worse than wasted should be spent in meditation and prayer. . . .

On Christ's coronation day He will not acknowledge as His any who bear spot or wrinkle or any such thing. But to His faithful ones He will give crowns of immortal glory.[57]

Ellen G. White

> We should live soberly, righteously, and godly, in this present world; looking for that blessed hope, and the glorious appearing of the great God and our Saviour Jesus Christ.
>
> Titus 2:12, 13.

In the Twinkling of an Eye

Awake and sing,

ye that dwell in dust:

for thy dew is as the

dew of herbs, and

the earth shall cast

out the dead.

Isaiah 26:19.

The King of kings descends upon the cloud, wrapped in flaming fire. The heavens are rolled together as a scroll, the earth trembles before Him, and every mountain and island is moved out of its place. . . .

Amid the reeling of the earth, the flash of lightning, and the roar of thunder, the voice of the Son of God calls forth the sleeping saints. He looks upon the graves of the righteous, then, raising His hands to heaven, He cries: "Awake, awake, awake, ye that sleep in the dust, and arise!" Throughout the length and breadth of the earth the dead shall hear that voice, and they that hear shall live. And the whole earth shall ring with the tread of the exceeding great army of every nation, kindred, tongue, and people. From the prison house of death they come, clothed with immortal glory, crying: "O death, where is thy sting? O grave, where is thy victory?" 1 Corinthians 15:55. And the living righteous and the risen saints unite their voices in a long, glad shout of victory.

All come forth from their graves the same in stature as when they entered the tomb. . . . But all arise with the freshness and vigor of eternal youth. . . . The mortal, corruptible form, devoid of comeliness, once polluted with sin, becomes perfect, beautiful, and immortal. All blemishes and deformities are left in the grave. . . .

The living righteous are changed "in a moment, in the twinkling of an eye." At the voice of God they were glorified; now they are made immortal and with the risen saints are caught up to meet their Lord in the air. Angels "gather together his elect from the four winds, from one end of heaven to the other."[58]

As the little infants come forth immortal from their dusty beds, they immediately wing their way to their mother's arms.[59]

Friends long separated by death are united, nevermore to part, and with songs of gladness ascend together to the City of God.[60]

Ellen G. White

Notes

[1] *Bible Echo*, Feb. 1, 1892.
[2] *The Desire of Ages* (Mountain View, Calif.: Pacific Press Pub. Assn., 1898), p. 313.
[3] *The Ministry of Healing* (Mountain View, Calif.: Pacific Press Pub. Assn., 1905), pp. 36, 37.
[4] Manuscript 95, 1898.
[5] Letter 84, 1900.
[6] *Review and Herald*, Oct. 27, 1885.
[7] *Youth's Instructor*, May 4, 1886.
[8] *The Adventist Home* (Nashville: Southern Pub. Assn., 1952), pp. 442, 443.
[9] *Child Guidance* (Nashville: Southern Pub. Assn., 1954), p. 475.
[10] Letter 73, 1905.
[11] Letter 41, 1877.
[12] Letter 97, 1895.
[13] Letter 8, 1873.
[14] *The Seventh-day Adventist Bible Commentary*, Ellen G. White Comments (Washington, D.C.: Review and Herald Pub. Assn., 1953-1957), vol. 4, p. 1183.
[15] *Ibid.*, vol. 7, p. 906.
[16] *Youth's Instructor*, Aug. 25, 1898.
[17] *Youth's Instructor*, Mar. 24, 1898.
[18] *Review and Herald*, Dec. 23, 1884.
[19] *Review and Herald*, Nov. 19, 1908.
[20] Letter 71, 1893.
[21] Manuscript 8, 1900.
[22] Manuscript 41, 1896.
[23] *Youth's Instructor*, September 1873.
[24] *Youth's Instructor*, July 14, 1892.
[25] *Youth's Instructor*, September 1873.
[26] *Youth's Instructor*, July 13, 1893.
[27] *Youth's Instructor*, February 1873.
[28] *Youth's Instructor*, July 13, 1893.
[29] *Review and Herald*, Nov. 1, 1892.
[30] *Child Guidance*, pp. 165, 166.
[31] *The Acts of the Apostles* (Mountain View, Calif.: Pacific Press Pub. Assn., 1911), p. 51.
[32] *Signs of the Times*, May 21, 1902.
[33] *The SDA Bible Commentary*, Ellen G. White Comments, vol. 6, pp. 1087, 1088.
[34] *Review and Herald*, Dec. 21, 1886.
[35] *Youth's Instructor*, June 10, 1897.
[36] *Review and Herald*, Dec. 29, 1910.
[37] Letter 1, 1904.
[38] *Child Guidance*, p. 424.
[39] *Ibid.*, pp. 423, 424.
[40] *Christ's Object Lessons* (Washington, D.C.: Review and Herald Pub. Assn., 1900), pp. 307-311.
[41] *That I May Know Him* (Washington, D.C.: Review and Herald Pub. Assn., 1964), p. 302.
[42] *Testimonies for the Church* (Mountain View, Calif.: Pacific Press Pub. Assn., 1948), vol. 5, pp. 220, 221.
[43] *Education* (Mountain View, Calif.: Pacific Press Pub. Assn., 1903), p. 249.
[44] *Testimonies*, vol. 2, pp. 478, 479.
[45] *Child Guidance*, p. 164.
[46] *Ibid.*, p. 165.
[47] *Ibid.*, pp. 165, 166.
[48] *Testimonies*, vol. 9, pp. 285, 286.
[49] *Ibid.*, p. 285.
[50] Undated manuscript 33.
[51] *Youth's Instructor*, May 4, 1893.
[52] Manuscript 39, 1895.
[53] *Christ's Object Lessons*, p. 232.
[54] Manuscript 168, 1902.
[55] *Youth's Instructor*, Jan. 3, 1895.
[56] *Youth's Instructor*, Jan. 25, 1910.
[57] *Review and Herald*, Nov. 24, 1904.
[58] *The Great Controversy* (Mountain View, Calif.: Pacific Press Pub. Assn., 1911), pp. 641-645.
[59] *Selected Messages* (Washington, D.C.: Review and Herald Pub. Assn., 1958, 1980), book 2, p. 260.
[60] *The Great Controversy*, p. 645.

More Family Reading

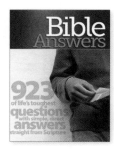

Bible Answers
You ask the questions; it points you to Bible texts with the answers

Lessons for Living
The true meaning hidden within the parables of Jesus

Beautiful in God's Eyes
Look into the eyes of your Creator and see the reflection of who you were meant to be, and find the kind of beauty that never fades.

Health Power
Choices you can make that will revolutionize your health

The New Life Challenge Cookbook
improve your family's health without compromising taste

Foods That Heal
A nutrition expert explains how to change your life by improving your diet

Plants That Heal
Unlocks the secrets of plants that heal the body and invigorate the mind

Seven Secrets Cookbook
Lose weight, lower cholesterol, reverse diabetes—healthy cuisine your family will love!

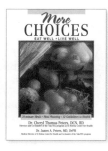

More Choices
All-natural meals you can make in 30 minutes

The Optimal Diet
The official CHIP cookbook, recipes to reverse and prevent lifestyle diseases

Fun With Kids In the Kitchen Cookbook
Let your kids help with these healthy recipes

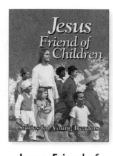

Jesus, Friend of Children
Favorite chapters from *The Bible Story*

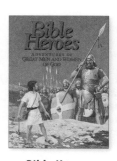

Bible Heroes
A selection of the most exciting adventures from *The Bible Story*

The Story Book
Excerpts from Uncle Arthur's *Bedtime Stories*

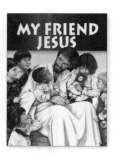

My Friend Jesus
Stories for preschoolers from the life of Christ, with activity pages

Home Health Education Service • P.O. Box 1119 • Hagerstown, MD 21741   www.thebiblestory.com

Books for the Entire Family to Enjoy

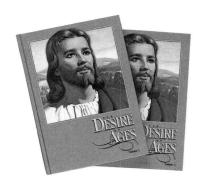

The Desire of Ages

This is E. G. White's monumental best seller on the life of Christ. It is perhaps the most spiritually perceptive of the Savior's biographies since the Gospel According to John. Here Jesus becomes more than a historic figure—He is the great divine-human personality set forth in a hostile world to make peace between God and humanity. Two volumes, hardcover.

Uncle Arthur's Bedtime Stories

For years this collection of stories has been the center of cozy reading experiences between parents and children. Arthur Maxwell tells the real-life adventures of young children—adventures that teach the importance of such character traits as kindness and honesty. Discover how a hollow pie taught Robert not to be greedy and how an apple pie shared by Annie saved her life. Five volumes, hardcover.

The Bible Story

This is the most accurate and complete set of children's Bible story books available. More than 400 Bible stories are included, with full-color paintings at every page opening. Unlike television, these stories introduce children to heroes you would be proud to have them imitate. These stories are also an excellent tool for loving parents who want their children to grow up making right decisions and making them with confidence. Ten volumes, hardcover.

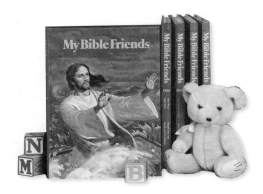

My Bible Friends

Imagine your child's delight as you read the charming story of Small Donkey, who carried tired Mary up the hill toward Bethlehem. Or of Zacchaeus the Cheater, who climbed a sycamore tree so he could see Jesus passing by. Each book has four attention-holding stories written in simple, crystal-clear language. And the colorful illustrations surpass in quality what you may have seen in any other children's Bible story book. Five volumes, hardcover. Also available in videos and audiocassettes.

A Woman's Devotional Time

Breathe
Ardis Dick Stenbakken

In a world demanding every ounce of who you are, do you ever feel as though you're losing yourself? Scheduling. Expectations. Relationships. Responsibilities. It might seem that you are required to be superhuman just to keep up.

And yet something inside you knows that just as your body can't survive without oxygen, your spirit also needs room to breathe—a well-deserved, guilt-free time-out from life's demands to refresh and reinspire your heart and mind.

Hardcover. 978-0-8280-2706-9

Prices and availability subject to change.
Canadian prices higher.